10 smart things women can do

to build a better life

Donna Carter

HARVEST HOUSE PUBLISHERS

EUGENE, OREGON

Back cover photo © Diane Diederich / iStockphoto

Back cover author photo © Andras Schram

Cover by Garborg Design Works, Savage, Minnesota

10 SMART THINGS WOMEN CAN DO TO BUILD A BETTER LIFE
Copyright © 2006 by Donna Carter
Published by Harvest House Publishers
Eugene, Oregon 97402
www.harvesthousepublishers.com

Library of Congress Cataloging-in-Publication Data
    Carter, Donna, 1961-
    10 smart things women can do to build a better life / Donna Carter.
        p. cm.
    ISBN-13: 978-0-7369-2039-1 (pbk.)
    ISBN-10: 0-7369-2039-0 (pbk.)
    1. Christian women—Religious life. 2. Self-actualization (Psychology) in women.
3. Self-actualization (Psychology)—Religious aspects—Christianity 4. Simplicity—Religious
aspects—Christianity. I. Title. II. Title: Ten smart things women can do to build a better life.
    BV4527.C28 2007
    248.8'43—dc22
                                                                          2007002515

Printed in the United States of America

09 10 11 12 13 14 15 / BP-SK / 12 11 10 9 8 7 6 5

Acknowledgments

I want to give credit to the many authors and experts whose works have been cited in this book. Their books and teachings have enriched my life and these pages.

Thanks also to my friends for allowing me to share their personal stories for the benefit of others. (I have given some of these individuals fictitious names to protect their privacy.)

Thanks to Don Bastian of Bastian Publishing Services, who began as my editor but became a cheerleader, advocate, and friend.

A huge thanks to Barbara Gordon of Harvest House Publishers for the great editorial work and to Terry Glaspey for the opportunity to play with the "big kids."

Thanks to Phil Callaway for doing whatever it was he did to get me on Harvest House's radar screen.

Also, thanks to the many generous friends and family members (you know who you are) who supported this project in various ways, from accommodating my preoccupation with this job to crafting proposals and proofreading.

Finally, thanks to the Straight Talk Board of Directors, subcommittee, and support base for believing in me. On my own I'd be about as effective as a two-wheeled tricycle. I trust that together we will help many women build better lives.

Contents

a note from donna

At the time of this writing I am 45 years old. I don't wish I was 35 or 25 or 15. When I had my photo taken for the back cover of this book, the photographer asked me what retouching I would like to have done to my face. I said none. This is not because I have no wrinkles or imperfections but because I wear my wrinkles as a badge of honor. I am grateful to have lived long enough on this planet to have some life experience to my name. I am also incredibly thankful for the abundance of smart and sensible people who have influenced me in countless ways. I have sat under the teaching of gifted teachers and pastors, read numerous brilliant authors, and been mentored by informed and discerning colleagues and friends. I have been raised by wise and loving parents and nurtured by supportive grandparents and other extended family members.

All of these people have contributed to the accumulated pool of distilled wisdom and experience that is now my own. It would be impossible for me to identify and separate what learning came from them and what thoughts are my own, since I have used the teaching of others as the foundation for my own ideas. So the wisdom I offer in *10 Smart Things Women Can Do to Build a Better Life* belongs as much to them as to me. They've allowed the influence of their lives to spill over into mine. It is my privilege to now allow the accumulated wisdom and insights to overflow and spill from my pool into yours.

Donna Carter

introduction

Have you ever had one of those *"Aha!"* moments when something suddenly becomes clear to you and you say to yourself, "I wish I had known this 10, 20, or 40 years ago. It would have changed everything. It would have set me free"? My hope is that this book will inspire these moments in your life.

10 Smart Things Women Can Do to Build a Better Life explores important issues we women wrestle with day to day. It draws from the learning of people with practical expertise and proven track records, as well as from what the Bible has to say on each of the 10 topics. It's unlikely that everyone who reads this book believes in the Bible as the flawless Word of God. Most people do, however, agree that it does contain a lot of wisdom. I also informally surveyed a large group of women, asking them about their "Aha!" moments and what they have learned that has helped them build better lives. From their answers and my own experiences, I have extracted 10 things that stand out as particularly transformational.

Thankfully, we don't have to learn everything the hard way. We can learn from other people's experiences. In fact, our public libraries are full of books based on just that premise. Following are some titles of how-to books (and I kid you not; these are real titles of real books).

~: *How to Attract the Wombat*

~: *How to Baby-sit an Orangutan*

~: *How to Catch an Elephant*

~: *How to Avoid Housework*
~: *How to be a Real Person in Just One Day*
~: *How to Be Funny*
~: *How to Be Poor*
~: *How to Be Not That Bad*
~: *How to Be Your Dog's Best Friend*
~: *How to Be Your Own Best Friend*

Don't you feel better knowing there is all that wisdom out there? While it is true that we often benefit from the wisdom of others, their opinions can confuse us as well. For instance, a man and his son were traveling to town. The father rode a donkey, and the boy walked along beside him. They met a man on the road who said to the father, "How can you ride in comfort on the back of that donkey while your son has to walk? Don't you see how unfair that is?"

If we fail to invest time and energy thinking through the important issues of life and deciding for ourselves how to live, we tend to do what everyone else is doing.

So the father and his son traded places.

A few miles down the road they encountered another traveler who said to the boy, "It is very disrespectful of you to allow your father to walk when you are riding on the back of a donkey. You should get down and let him ride."

So the man and his son traded places again.

A little while later they were approached by a third traveler. He said, "How inhumane of you to ride on the back of that little donkey. He is obviously very tired, and you are both able to walk on your own."

When last seen, the man and the boy were carrying the donkey down the road.

As ridiculous as that may sound, you and I could easily find ourselves in a similar situation. If we fail to invest time and energy thinking through the important issues of life and deciding for ourselves how to live, we will tend to do what everyone else is doing or follow the advice of the most recent "guru" appearing on popular talk shows.

The quality of the choices we make today will be reflected in the quality of our lives tomorrow. So please read this book with an open mind and an open heart. Spend some time reflecting on the questions at the end of each chapter. Or better yet, discuss them in a group of friends. I believe that if you do these things, *10 Smart Things Women Can Do to Build a Better Life* will help you lock on to your true values and help you decide how you want to live. You will find practical tools you can use to make positive changes in your life.

Are you ready to explore what you can do to create a better life? All right! Let's dig in.

1

make space

*How can I organize my life so I have time, money,
and energy to focus on what's important?*

Have you ever had one of those days when you were 20 minutes late for a dinner engagement, because you were 15 minutes late picking your kids up from school, because you were 10 minutes late at the hairdresser, because you were 5 minutes late leaving the office?

Have you ever suffered the humiliation of having to leave some of your groceries at the checkout counter because you impulsively spent your grocery money on a really cute shirt?

Have you ever finished the day with no energy and yet you still had a ton of work to do before you could crash for the night?

Have you ever pretended you couldn't hear your child calling because you couldn't face one more demand?

Whether we're talking about time concerns, money management, or the crowding of our energy and emotions, we are really dealing with space issues. What do I mean? Occasionally, in my previous work as an interior designer, I had clients who were determined to use every good decorating idea they ever saw...all in one room. I had to explain an interesting principle: that over-decorating creates chaos out of what could be stunningly beautiful. Just because a space has been left unfilled *does not* mean it has been left undesigned.

Interior designers call strategically unfilled areas "negative space." Negative space is very important. It contributes to the beauty of a room by creating a sense of order and restfulness. It allows the eye the freedom to find the elements in the room that really deserve attention: a beautiful sculpture, a cozy fireplace, a breathtaking view.

In today's obsession with speed, chaos, and clutter, employing negative space in our lives can create order and peace. It also enables us to place priorities on the facets of our lives that really matter.

Drawing on Richard Swenson's book *Margin* and Bill Hybels' *Watching Your Gauges,* I've highlighted five major areas of life in which we all need space left empty by design. To assess how you are doing at making space in all the right places, imagine the control center of your life as a dashboard with five gauges on it. Women who check these gauges and stay out of the red zones dramatically reduce their daily stress levels, keep themselves out of serious trouble, and, in the long term, build better lives.

Your Time Gauge

My husband and I went to Malaysia a few years ago. We traveled through six airports going and six returning. An interesting fact we learned on our long journey is that airports are required by law to leave extra time between international flights. This is to accommodate the inevitable delays and complications of world travel. Missing a plane on our tight schedule would have put me right over the edge, so I was glad this was in place. Still, after 30 hours in planes and airports, a 4-hour wait in the Los Angeles airport in the middle of the night wasn't my idea of a good time.

Contrast that experience to our trip home from the Dominican Republic last year. In Toronto we had a connection time that, although it fell within legal limits, was completely inadequate for clearing customs, traversing a huge airport, and waiting in security lines. Recognizing we were under time pressure, our trip coordinator bolted from the plane and secured a place in a customs line.

Then, as each one of our group emerged from the crowd, she waved us over and let us cut in. Needless to say, this did not endear us to the people already in line. We apologized to the grumbling travelers but held our ground. Once through customs, we grabbed our bags and sprinted through the corridors of Pearson International toward the security line.

Because we were a group of nine travelers, customs had taken extra time, and the same people who had complained about our line etiquette were now ahead of us in this line. We knew we still had a shuttle ride ahead of us and our next flight was leaving shortly. I boldly went to the front of the line and explained our situation to the security guard. He graciously waved us all to the front of the line.

Now, you have to realize how uncomfortable this was for a group of Canadians, who as a nation are known for being unfailingly (even ridiculously) polite. My husband, in offering another round of apologies to the same disgruntled passengers we had cut ahead of before, somehow got separated from the rest of the group. His instructions to me were, "Whether I make it or not, get on the plane." So together with our daughters, Kendall and Kevann, I made a break for the shuttle. Once on the bus, we breathlessly pleaded with the driver to wait for my husband. A tall, broad shadow appeared behind the airport doors. I said, "I'm sure this is him now. Please wait." The airport doors parted, and a large man emerged. He was not my husband. The doors closed. "Please wait just another minute," I begged the driver. Another shadow appeared behind the doors. They parted and Randy appeared. The girls shouted, "Run, Daddy, run!" Randy sprinted to the shuttle. He pried the closing doors open and dragged himself inside. Everyone on the shuttle cheered. This trip was proving more stressful than the *Amazing Race!* Why would anyone willingly put themselves through that?

Unfortunately, we do similar things to ourselves all the time. We hustle and rush to make appointments, get to work, drop off kids, and more. But we can bring a degree of sanity into our lives simply by making space in the way we plan our days. Instead of being stressed out because something took longer than it should have, we can anticipate that not everything will go as expected and plan accordingly.

Our Creator knows we need down time. God devised a law to allow negative space in our lives. It's called the Sabbath (observed by most Jews on Saturday and by most Christians on Sunday), and it's recorded in the Ten Commandments (Exodus 20:8-10):

> Remember to observe the Sabbath day by keeping it holy. Six days a week are set apart for your daily duties and regular work, but the seventh day is a day of rest dedicated to the LORD your God. On that day no one in your household may do any kind of work.

Now that may seem heavy-handed and restrictive, but in reality it is a gift. In giving it, God was saying to his people, "Let everyone around you work themselves into the ground. I want a better life for you. I want to give you the gift of rest. Go ahead and work hard for six days, but then take a day off. Enjoy each other and celebrate me. In the end, you will be amazed at how much more productive you are."

God wants us to take a day off. He created us and he knows we need it physically, emotionally, relationally, and spiritually.

Research from the business world confirms that God knew what he was doing (no surprise there). Karen Hanna, a former vice president of Levi Strauss and currently a life coach, has determined that people are at peak effectiveness when they take 120 days off per year. This equates to two days off per week plus three weeks of vacation.

Interesting, isn't it, that keeping the Sabbath is the only one of the 10 suggestions...oops, I mean commandments...that we see as optional? We pretty much agree that murder, lying, and stealing are not good things, but taking a day off? Not so much. Stranger still is that we often feel guiltier for not working on Sunday in violation of our culture's values than we do when we do work on Sunday in violation of God's values.

Workaholism may be applauded and rewarded by the workaday world, and some would argue that it paves the path to success, but God says it's wrong, whether our work is in the home or outside. He wants us to take a day off. He created us, and he knows we need it physically, emotionally, relationally, and spiritually. It's a commandment designed to make us more effective and available to the people around us and to help us build better lives.

You may be thinking, "Well, if I don't do the laundry on Sunday, when else can I possibly do it?" The answer is that you likely have more discretionary time than you think. Maybe you're lazy... Now you're thinking, *Okay, now I'm offended. Them's fightin' words.* But don't shoot me yet. Laziness, as it is defined in the Bible, refers not only to idleness but also to preoccupation with the insignificant. Does this seem more plausible? Here are some suggestions for combating potential time-wasters:

- ~: Turn off the TV (the average person spends 20 to 30 hours per week watching)
- ~: Learn how to say no to the things that should not be on your agenda at this time
- ~: Get off the phone and off the Net (use them as tools, not as entertainment)
- ~: Stay out of the mall

If we are monitoring our time gauge, we will deliberately create negative space in our schedules. That allows us time to nurture ourselves and our relationships, thus improving life for ourselves and everyone close to us.

Your Emotional Gauge

Several years ago my husband and I were on the summer staff of Green Bay Bible Camp, a first-class Christian camping resort located on Lake Okanagan in beautiful British Columbia. Our jobs were to be resources to the staff. This included spending every afternoon on the beach talking to people. Doesn't that sound rough? Basking in the sun while engaging in conversation? Physically it was wonderful. But emotionally it was hard. Really hard.

I remember taking off one afternoon to go out for lunch with a woman I know who lives near the camp. I was so looking forward to some light conversation and a good laugh after all the heavy issues and heart pain I had been dealing with. But we had barely sat down at the table when she began telling me how devastated she was because of all the terrible stuff going on in her life. I wanted to scream, "No! I don't want to hear your problems. I don't care if you're in pain. I want you to make me laugh. *NOW!*"

One way we know our emotional tank is empty is when we begin to resent people for having needs: our babies for being dependent, our parents for getting sick, our husbands for wanting intimacy. Unless we are constantly refilling our tank, we will frequently get to the place where we just don't have the emotional fuel to care for anyone or about anything else.

How do you refuel your emotional life? Figure out what replenishes you. For me it's walking in a park and drinking in the serenity of nature. For my husband it's anything that involves noise, speed, and smoke. Everyone is different. Figure out what you need and how often you need it—and then schedule it in.

My husband crashed at the end of that summer at Green Bay. A visit to the doctor confirmed that he was experiencing the inevitable result of no physical and emotional space: depression. I realize there are many ways into depression, and for some it is a very long and difficult path out. For Randy, it wasn't until he allowed himself some time in the bush on a motorbike with friends that he began to come out of it. It is not selfish to allow yourself space. It is necessary for your emotional health.

Your Energy Gauge

Our physical energy is dependant on a combination of the oxygen we breathe, the food we take in as fuel, the demands we make on our bodies, the opportunity for recovery through sleep, and our general level of physical fitness. With that in mind, envision the typical, time-challenged woman. She reluctantly starts her engine some time around six-thirty in the morning with a strong cup of coffee, which keeps her running smoothly enough to make herself presentable, get the kids out the door, and take herself to work. Her overcrowded morning is powered by a few more cups of bad office coffee or, if she is lucky, a latte from the corner cafe. By lunchtime her body is seriously dehydrated and vibrating from all the caffeine she's consumed. Her blood sugar has plummeted because it has taken in no actual fuel today (unless she was lucky enough to score a latte).

Ah, but that's where the Hostess Twinkies come in. Not having time for lunch and being the quintessential, harried-but-efficient woman, she has had the forethought to stock her desk drawer with them. An hour into the afternoon she has a headache and a deep longing to crawl under her desk for a nap. No time for that. Better have another cup of coffee instead.

By the time she gets home from work, she is short-tempered, frazzled, trembling noticeably...and ravenous. Far too hungry to delay eating until supper, she removes the boxes and cans that hold supper from the pantry while she snacks on handfuls of Oreos and random sugared cereal bits left on the counter from the kids' breakfasts.

By the time her canned and cardboard supper is served and consumed, homework and music or sports practicing rituals have been observed and enforced, and children are filed for the night, her fuel deficit becomes impossible to ignore. She spends the rest of the evening grazing on whatever she can get her lips around, going from one poor excuse for food to another. And because her body is demanding real nutrition, nothing is really satisfying her.

Tomorrow she will do it all again, all the while wondering why she always seems to have a headache, has trouble sleeping, is edgy and irritable, and continues to gain weight. After all, she only eats one meal a day!

Okay, maybe most of us aren't that bad. But many of us can identify with those tendencies. It's amazing how little relationship most people see between their physical performance and what they consume for fuel. Many women keep the pace of an Olympic athlete, but instead of powering their aggressive approach to life with protein and complex carbohydrates, they survive on caffeine and complex schedules. And then they wonder why their physical energy gauge is constantly reading low.

In addition to being poorly nourished, we are sleep deprived. In the 1850s, adults were getting nine-and-a-half hours of sleep per night. Medical science tells us this is the optimum. When the lightbulb was invented, that amount of time began to decline. Today the average night's sleep is seven hours—and it's still decreasing. Maybe, just maybe, God knew what he was doing in making it dark all night.

Yes, we can schedule our time down to the millisecond, but if we don't manage our physical energy by allowing sufficient recovery time through sleep, we can't do our best work and we have nothing left to give to those we love. Another consequence is that vacations become, out of dire necessity, a time to recuperate instead of a time to play, which we also need. It turns out energy, not time, is our most precious resource.

Until his retirement, my dad worked as a corporate attorney. Lawyers are notorious workaholics. Yet even in an oil boomtown like Calgary, my dad rarely worked overtime. To say that choice put him in the minority of lawyers working in the oil and gas industry is something close to the understatement of the ages.

I didn't know until I had grown up and become acquainted with many other lawyers what an anomaly it was to have a dad in that profession who was available to his wife, his children, and his community on evenings and weekends. But understanding that made some of his idiosyncrasies make sense. It had long been a family joke that Dad was preprogrammed to go to bed at eleven o'clock. We speculated on what would happen if my parents were hosting guests who stayed past eleven on a weeknight. Would Dad just disappear and go to bed whether the party raged on or not? We never found out.

We did know that if one of the board meetings he attended continued until late, Dad could be counted on to excuse himself at eleven. He was absolutely religious about it. But here's the thing: Because he knew how to manage his physical energy, he was extraordinarily productive for those eight or nine hours per day he spent at the office. And since he wasn't the least bit interested in keeping his chair warm simply to impress the oil baron brass, there was no reason to stay at the office any longer than that. Because he knew how much sleep he required to perform optimally in a demanding and vitally important position in his company, he considered it stealing from his employer to go to work sleep deprived.

Monitoring our physical energy gauge means we establish and maintain a lifestyle that includes a healthful diet, adequate sleep, and exercise.

Everything we do, think, and feel costs us energy. Certainly some chapters of life are much greedier with our physical resources than others. I remember feeling incredibly depleted after the death of a close friend. I had my own interior design consulting business at the time, and because I was working to finish a large retail store in another city in preparation for their grand opening event, I had little opportunity for down time to process my grief. I remember working the day after my friend died, during part of the day of her funeral, and for all the days in between. I felt confused about my exhaustion. I didn't understand the physical demands that grieving was placing on my body.

Any mother of preschoolers knows the physical cost of keeping up with little people day after day. Whoever decided it should always be the stay-at-home parent who gets up with children in the night because the "breadwinner" has to get up and go to *work* needs to refine their definition of work. If you've done both jobs, you no doubt agree that it's far more physically demanding to stay at home with small children than it is to go to an office and deal with adults.

Creating space in our physical energy means we balance times of high energy demand with a proportionate amount of rest. There are times for all of us when we have to put the pedal to the metal. Businesspeople and students have deadlines. Parents have periods of time when they don't get breaks because their partners are unavailable or they have no partners. But if we don't allow for space to recover from times of high demand, our bodies will eventually protest. Usually that revolt takes the form of a compromised immune system that becomes vulnerable to every virus or bacteria in the neighborhood. Over time that susceptibility can become much more serious and debilitating.

Even when we're sleeping enough and eating well, if we are not challenging our hearts, lungs, and muscles, we aren't giving ourselves enough space. I don't particularly enjoy exercising, and I don't really understand people who do enjoy it. There is a woman who exercises at the gym with me who loves working out. She really loves it! Personally, I think she needs counseling. I work out because I like the ways I benefit from it: My mood is elevated, my hormones regulated, my bones and muscles consolidated, my stress mitigated, and my fat incinerated.

Monitoring our physical energy gauge means we establish and maintain a lifestyle that includes a healthful diet and adequate sleep and exercise. The cost is outweighed by the benefit: increased energy and a greater sense of well-being.

Your Financial Gauge

Overspending has become the norm. Not only does the typical family crowd out all available space in their finances, they borrow space they don't have. According to American Consumer Credit Counseling, the average American carries a credit card debt load of $8,562! On top of that mountain, people also assume debts for vehicles, furniture, vacations, and more. Often when we ask ourselves whether or not we can afford something, what we really mean is, "Can we afford the payments?"

This is a huge problem because when we have no unused space in our financial world, spending crowds out other areas of our lives.

Early in our marriage, Randy and I decided we would never make a major purchase without discussing it and sleeping on it. This has saved us countless mistakes. What seems like a bargain that's too-good-to-be-true while standing in a car lot, or a furniture store, or sitting eyeball to eyeball with a skilled salesperson, often reverts to an extravagance we can't really afford once reality sets in. I hate to think of the debt I would have brought on my family if my love of shopping and equal love of beautiful things were the only deciding factors in my spending.

> *Space in our finances enables us to invest generously in the lives of others whose needs are greater than our own. It also prepares us for a rainy day.*

Impulse buying is often the main culprit in problem spending. We see something we want but can't really afford...so we buy it anyway. Then we have to work longer hours to pay off our credit cards. As a result, we are emotionally and physically exhausted. We're far too tired to exercise or build relationships.

Do you see where this is going? Into a downward spiral of excess.

We need to simplify our lives by buying less. We need to let our values—not our desire for status, or our lack of restraint, or even our income—determine our lifestyle. In his book *Little House on the Freeway,* Tim Kimmel writes:

> There seems to be a direct relationship between a person's heart and his checkbook. When a couple decides to settle for a certain standard and stop chasing the Joneses all over town, they experience a rest in their work and in their home that no higher standard of living could supply.
>
> It takes courage to make the choice to be satisfied. It takes courage to invest the excess in others when you could be indulging yourself. It takes courage to say no to wants that would only complicate your life. But the reward of inner rest is worth it.

Years ago I heard the story of a wealthy man's son who approached his dad for the money to buy a very expensive pair of jeans. The father denied the son's request. The son asked, "Why not, Dad? We can afford it." The father wisely answered, "Son, we can afford to buy not only those jeans, but also the store selling them and the mall where the store is located. That is not the point. The point is that we have chosen to spend conservatively on ourselves so that we can be generous with others."

That's value-driven spending. Space in our finances enables us to invest generously in the lives of others whose needs are greater than our own. It also prepares us for rainy days.

What is the worst thing that can happen if you continue to live with no financial space in your life? You'll be in debt up to your eyeballs but too busy, tired, and depressed to care. But worse than that, life will become all about going to work and spending money and digesting food and watching sitcoms and drifting into unconsciousness just in time to wake up and do it all over again. That's not living; that's existing.

Your Spiritual Gauge

What is the purpose of life? The Westminster Catechism answers that question when it states that "the chief end of man is to glorify God and enjoy Him forever." In other words, we are on this planet to worship God and be his friends. If this is true, then to live without faith is to completely miss the point of being here.

We are physical, intellectual, social, and spiritual beings. If we ignore the spiritual aspect of our lives, we're in for a rough ride. Study after study reports that people of faith are healthier, have happier marriages, and live longer. We were created to find fulfillment in relationship with our Creator. When we deny this reality, we lack ultimate purpose.

Some people describe this condition as a God-shaped hole that he has intentionally placed inside us. He wants us to long for him just as he longs for us. When we fill up our spiritual tank by pursuing a relationship with him, we find contentment that is unparalleled by anything else.

That God-shaped hole is filled by God's own Spirit when we invite him into our lives. We keep the tank full by spending time talking to God through prayer, reading his love letter to us (the Bible), and learning about him from people who know him well. In applying what we learn to our lives, we live as our Creator designed us to live. We find out just how rich life can be!

From time to time we all visit red zones. But if any one of your gauges is in the red on a regular basis, you are spatially challenged. There's no shame in that. These are complex issues. It's hard to create and maintain negative space because it requires a lot of self-discipline and vigilant monitoring. But the sanity gained is well worth it.

Watching the gauges of our time, physical energy, emotional energy, and finances and taking action when necessary enable us to live with unfilled space in the first four areas of our lives. It ensures that we have the resources we need to get where we want to go. Monitoring that final gauge of our spirit helps us determine where that is.

You can build a better life by watching your gauges and keeping out of the red. Enjoy the spaciousness and freedom that result!

— *Making Space* —

1. Are you a workaholic? Would your close friends, spouse, and kids agree with your answer?

2. Do you feel guiltier when you work on Sunday or when you don't?

3. In what ways are you "preoccupied with the insignificant"?

4. What recharges your emotional energy? How often do you do it?

5. Do you protect your physical energy? Brainstorm ways to stay balanced in this area.

6. Do you agree or disagree with the Tim Kimmel quote about the relationship between the heart and the checkbook (between financial space and satisfaction)? Why?

7. Are you on overload? What changes do you need to make in your time, emotional energy, physical energy, and finances?

8. How is your spiritual gauge reading these days?

2

manage emotions

*How can I relate to people in a positive way
even when they push my buttons?*

Our emotional world is one of the most difficult parts of our lives to manage. We think we're in complete control, but then something or someone pushes our buttons and our emotions go from 0 to 60 faster than a Porsche. Later, in the aftermath, we wonder, "What was that all about?"

Surging emotions create all kinds of problems for us, but we wouldn't want to be without them. What physical sensation is to the physical body, emotions are to the heart. They warn us when our souls are in danger and calm us when they are safe. Removing this God-given warning system would be like taking away the body's ability to feel pain. We could become badly damaged before we realize something is wrong.

Let me give you an example. My husband is the macho, action-oriented type. Randy's never met an extreme sport he didn't like. He is so competitive and so completely involved in the game or task at hand that he becomes temporarily immune to pain. *Temporarily.*

One day he was playing hockey when his face had an unfortunate, unscheduled meeting with another player's shoulder pad, which opened a significant gash under Randy's left eye. Presumably the combination of the cold air temperature at the rink and

Randy's refusal to acknowledge his injury kept him from bleeding all over the ice. When the game was over, he showered and dressed and started driving to an appointment. Suddenly a trickle of blood started coursing down his cheek. He dabbed it with a tissue. The trickle quickly became a gush, and the gush, a torrent.

In the middle of rush-hour traffic, there was Randy frantically groping through the car for anything remotely absorbent to stem the tide of blood. In sheer desperation he settled for a sweaty sock from his hockey bag. It was now clear that he wasn't going anywhere until he stopped at the emergency room of a nearby hospital to have the gash stitched shut.

Ignoring or being numb to pain—physical or emotional—isn't healthy. It prevents us from responding appropriately to the people and the situations in our lives that can cause us harm. Learning to read our emotions as the warning system they are and determining what our emotional reactions are telling us are critical. This is how we can evaluate whether our hearts truly are in danger in the present moment or if there is something more complicated happening. Only then can we respond appropriately to what is going on around us and inside us. Only then can we keep an isolated overreaction from becoming a predictable pattern.

I grew up in a relatively frugal home. My dad was a successful professional and money was not in short supply, but we definitely lived by the adage of "Waste not, want not." I'll never forget something that happened once when Dad came into the house after cutting the lawn. Because he was trying to avoid spreading grass clippings in the house, he carried his shoes in his hands as he tiptoed past the kitchen table, which was set for supper. At precisely the wrong moment, the shoes slipped out of his hands. One of them headed with the precision of a guided missile toward a full pitcher of milk on the table. The projectile landed gloriously inside the pitcher with a dramatic splash.

My sister and I saw the whole episode unfold in slow motion. We were faced with an enormous challenge: controlling our laughter without turning ourselves inside out. Holding our mirth was necessary because we knew, even before seeing the angry expression on our gentle dad's face, that he would fail to see the humor of the situation. We knew, in fact, that what to us was first-class slapstick comedy would be to him—someone who grew up during the Great Depression—a grievous waste of food.

Why do we sometimes have mountainous reactions to molehills of problems? Good question. It happens to all of us, doesn't it? Your child does some typical kid thing, and you unleash an angry response completely out of proportion to the crime committed. Your boss overlooks you for a promotion, and the rejection you feel penetrates right down to the bone. You see someone who reminds you of a dark figure in your past, and the fear stops you in your tracks. The emotional reaction brought on by events like these is seldom a result of the event or trigger alone. There is something going on beneath the surface.

De Boat Is de Problem

Our emotions are like indicator lights on the dashboard of a car. When the oil light goes on, it isn't telling us there is something wrong with the light. The light is telling us there is trouble under the hood. If all you do when the light goes on is yank out cables under the dash until the light goes out, you have only dealt with the indicator that something is wrong. A short distance down the road you will have more significant trouble to deal with than if you had dealt with the real problem when you were first alerted to it.

Our emotions are not the problem; they are the indication of a problem. Several years ago my husband and I traveled to Haiti to meet two of the children we sponsor through a wonderful child-development organization called Compassion. Part of the trip involved a boat ride to an island called La Gonave, off the west coast. The trip to the island was uneventful. The trip back was anything but. Our first clue that things were not going according to plan was when the boats that Compassion's field office had hired for the return trip didn't show up. We waited two hours before two other boats arrived. One looked quite acceptable; the other looked highly questionable.

Knowing we couldn't stay on the island indefinitely, we got into the boats. By the way all of us wanted to pile into the good boat, you'd have thought it was a lifeboat on the *Titanic*. My husband and I, trying to be considerate, ended up in the other boat. It was old and filthy and had too few life jackets to go around. It did sport two outboard motors, one of which was tied—yes, tied—onto the back.

> *By the time we reach maturity, we have feelings about every topic, every place, every event because we've been colored and informed by our experiences.*

"If one of those motors dies, we're toast," my husband Randy muttered. He shouldn't have said it. Not 10 minutes later, one of the motors died, and none of the efforts of our three-man Haitian crew could revive it. Our boat, no longer able to hydroplane, sank sluggishly into the water. This meant that with every wave the Caribbean sent our way, water sloshed over the side of the boat, soaking us and slowly filling our woeful conveyance.

At this point I was being a good sport and kind of enjoying the adventure. Randy, on the other hand, who is by nature far more skilled at adventure than I am, recognized the trouble we were in. He began to bail water. While he bailed, he noticed that salt water was pouring into our gas supply. However, because of the noise of the boat and spray (not to mention his inability to speak Creole), he couldn't communicate the problem to the crew. For the duration of our little Caribbean "cruise," while my friend Karen and I prayed, Randy held the ill-fitting lid of the gas container down with one hand and furiously bailed with the other.

It was a good thing Randy was with us or we never would have made it to shore. Though our Haitian crew members were not great problem-solvers, they did recognize we had a significant problem. They headed for the closest point of terra firma, which was far from the place where our vehicle and the rest of our team were waiting. We didn't care. We were just so glad to make land. Any land. As we tried to wring the seawater from our hair and clothes, our guide, a Haitian pastor, patiently debriefed us, saying, "De ocean is not de problem. De boat is de problem."

When it comes to our emotions, what at first glance appears to be the problem is seldom the real trouble. When we experience strong emotions like frustration, anger, and fear, there is usually something going on under the surface. Something we need to investigate. De emotion is not de problem...something else is de problem.

Like the Haitian boat crew, we often try to deal with the symptoms of the problem (bailing de ocean) without searching for the real cause (de boat). The underlying problem is our emotional conditioning. By the time we reach maturity, we have had all sorts of experiences that have become integrated into our perspective and affect the way we perceive life. We have feelings about every topic, every place, every event because we've been colored and informed by our experiences.

Many years ago, while watching the evening news, I was reduced to tears in a matter of seconds by the image of an ultrasound scan on the television. Had I been in the company of anyone who didn't know me well, I would have had some explaining to do. I can't tell you what the featured news story was about now. All I remember is the powerful effect that image had on me. My sensitivity had nothing to do with the story being presented; it had everything to do with the fact that the one and only time an ultrasound was prescribed for me personally, it revealed what the doctor already suspected. The child I carried in my womb was dead. The grief of that moment when the devastating truth became obvious to everyone focused on that monitor came rushing back to me. Power-ful emotions flowed like turbulent water rushing through a narrow canyon as I sat unsuspectingly watching the evening news.

When we feel intense emotion that is out of proportion to the present catalyst, we need to "look under the hood" to discern what past event or experience is coloring the present. Once we know the cause of our exaggerated emotion, we can manage it.

When I was a teenager, I took singing lessons from a woman who grew up in England during the Second World War. She had been severely scarred emotionally by the terror of the bombings she had survived as a little girl. One horrible night will live forever in her memory. She was awakened during an electrical storm by the awful percussion of an explosion and the frantic shouts of adults and cries of children. The German Luftwaffe had dropped a bomb near her home, and flames surrounded her and her family.

They all escaped the fire by running through the storm to the home of some friends. The traumatized family hunkered down to wait out the bombing, the storm, and the night. But before the thunder stopped rumbling or dawn could come, another bomb exploded nearby, once again starting a fire and stealing their shelter.

I didn't know any of this when, in the middle of a music lesson, my 55-year-old teacher landed in my lap at the first crack of thunder announcing the arrival of a storm. Why the strong reac-tion? Because, to her, every storm signified danger, every boom was a bomb, and every flash of light was an explosion. Didn't she know the threat was not the same in the present as it had been in the past? Her head knew it, but her head failed to inform her heart.

She's About to Blow!

We are completely incapable of controlling our *instantaneous* emotional reaction to an event. But we can quickly manage those emotions by teaching our heads to talk to our hearts. When our heads tell our hearts the truth, we can bring an emotional volcano under control so that the response is a squirt of steam and not an eruption of lava.

How does the head inform the heart? Consider this example. You've just left a job after 12 years of bashing your head against a glass ceiling that is dripping with testosterone. You have been disrespected, disregarded, and passed over in every possible way because you are female. You have brought all those years of frustration and anger into a new job that you took great pains to be sure was estrogen friendly.

You and your mostly male team have just finished a really great presentation, and you are feeling very pleased with yourself. That is, until your boss individually thanks all the members of the team except you. He meant to thank everyone equally. He genuinely appreciates you. Excluding you was a simple oversight. But your previous work experience has set the lava to boiling. If you were able to think coherently at all, you would yell out, "Get out of the way, boys, she's about to blow!"

This is your gut reaction. It's that immediate, visceral, unmeasured emotional response. The next thing that must take place if the eruption is to be avoided is a sensible conversation between your head and your heart. You see, your head knows that based on everything

> *The way the story ends depends on what you tell yourself in that moment. Telling yourself the objective truth enables you to manage your emotions.*

you painstakingly researched about this man and your own brief experience with him, he is not sexist. You know that he values your contribution to the organization equally to those of the men on your team. You know that the only explanation for what happened is a brain hiccup.

While your lungs suck air in and blow it out, your head tells your heart the truth. Gradually your adrenal glands back off and the hammering of your heart calms down. The decrease in volatility that you are feeling enables you to refrain from lambasting your boss, who is blissfully unaware that he has offended you. He doesn't get accosted; you don't get fired or go to jail. Everyone wins.

This story could have a very different ending. You might have let your careening emotions do your thinking for you. You could have told yourself:

~: "I knew this would happen."

~: "He's just like all the other men I've worked with."

~: "It's impossible for a woman to get ahead in the workplace."

~: "All men are jerks."

This would have added more baggage to the convoy you already drag along behind you, making you even more firmly entrenched in your belief that all men are chauvinists. Then you may have blown up at your boss, ending a career with an employer who really valued you.

The way the story ends depends not on what pushes your buttons to evoke an emotional response but on what you tell yourself in that moment. What you say to yourself determines what happens next. Telling yourself the objective truth enables you to manage your emotions. The truth in this situation?

~: "My boss is not sexist."

~: "Excluding me was nothing more than an oversight."

~: "He values me as much as he does his male employees."

~: "This is a good job."

~: "I have the power to control myself and keep my job."

In his letter to the Philippians in the New Testament, the apostle Paul writes: "Fix your thoughts on what is true and honorable and right. Think about things that are pure and lovely and admirable.

Think about things that are excellent and worthy of praise" (4:8). He wrote that nearly 2,000 years ago. Today, psychologist William Backus, among others, calls the apostle's advice "Misbelief Therapy: Learning to replace our wrong or exaggerated impressions with the truth." When we employ this biblical strategy for managing our emotions, we first have to figure out the lies that build the seismic pressure inside of us. Then we can diffuse those emotional bombs by identifying, personalizing, and expressing the truth as it applies to each situation we encounter. For example:

~: "I'm such a loser" becomes "Okay, that was a stupid mistake, but I am smart enough to learn from my mistakes. I am still a person of worth."

~: "I'm so ugly" turns into "I'm not the most beautiful woman in the room, but I have beautiful qualities most of these people know nothing about. Those who know me appreciate the beauty in me."

~: "I can't do anything right" may be replaced by "This is clearly not my area of strength, but I'm proud of myself for trying. There are things I do very well."

~: "I'm powerless" becomes "I am not a child anymore. The perspective and skills I've gained over the years have empowered me to deal with this situation decisively and effectively."

Getting Real with God

Our emotions are products of our thought life. In reality we have very little direct control over our emotions, but we can control our thoughts. Replacing the confidence-killing, joy-sucking, rage-detonating lies in our minds with the truth calms our hearts. This doesn't mean the negative emotion disappears. It just becomes manageable. The next step is to tell God the truth.

There are basically three possible options for processing our strong emotions. First, we can suppress them, pushing them down where they will eat away at us and make us miserable. That is self-destructive. Second, we can explode all over everyone around us, wounding them and making the people we love miserable. That is also destructive. Third, we can vent our emotions to God. He has broad shoulders. He can absorb our outburst without our relationship sustaining any damage. In fact, the opposite is true. He *wants* us to come to him with our fragile hearts exposed. And it's not as if we can hide the truth from God anyway. By choosing to come to him with our hearts vulnerable, by telling him how we are feeling, we invite him into our experience much as we would unload after a bad day by talking to our moms, husbands, or girlfriends.

Listen to this very "unholy" prayer from Psalm 109, in which Israel's King David dumps on God:

> O God, whom I praise,
>   don't stand silent and aloof while the wicked slander
>   me....
>
> Arrange for an evil person to turn on him.
>   Send an accuser to bring him to trial.
>
> When his case is called for judgment,
>   let him be pronounced guilty.
>
> Count his prayers as sins.
>
> Let his years be few;
>   let his position be given to someone else.
>
> May his children become fatherless,
>   and may his wife become a widow.
>
> May his children wander as beggars;
>   may they be evicted from their ruined homes.
>
> May creditors seize his entire estate,
>   and strangers take all he has earned.
>
> Let no one be kind to him;
>   let no one pity his fatherless children.
>
> May all his offspring die.

> May his family name be blotted out
> in a single generation.

> May the LORD never forget the sins of his ancestors;
> may his mother's sins never be erased from the
> record... (verses 1-2,6-14).

David's not finished yet, but I think you get the point. There's nothing noble or holy about his prayer. It's just real. Very real. And I think that's why God made sure it ended up in the Bible. David went on many of these little tirades before God. And still God called David a man after his own heart. God wants us to be real with him, and he wants to make himself real to us. He does that when we take our angry, frustrated, broken hearts to him. As Psalm 34:18 says, "The LORD is close to the brokenhearted; he rescues those who are crushed in spirit."

When we know we can go to God with our strong emotions and be heard, understood, accepted, and comforted, we don't have to dump on everyone else. And when we tell ourselves the truth, we manage our emotions by responding to reality instead of reacting to our own subjective version of it.

Trying to function while at the mercy of our mood swings day after day is frustrating, complicated, and erratic. Managing our emotions makes life easier for everyone.

— *Managing Emotions* —

1. What types of situations really push your buttons?

2. Have you ever wondered why you overreact to certain circumstances? How do you explain this to yourself?

3. Can you detect a link between your strong emotional reactions and your emotional conditioning (how your experiences have shaped you)? Describe it.

4. How can you reduce the intensity of your emotional reaction when your buttons are pushed? Give an example of what that might look like for you.

5. What do you think of King David's "unholy prayer"? Can you imagine talking to God like that? Why or why not?

6. What happens when you tell God the truth about how you feel?

7. How would your life improve if you managed your emotions better?

3

concede control

How can I stop trying to control the universe?

Do you like to be in control? Do you do the driving whether you are in the driver's seat or not? Are your spices alphabetized? Do you tell your husband how to put the children to bed? Do you hate when things don't go as planned?

To some degree we all like to be in control, but this is more intense for some people than others. My elder daughter is a strong-willed child. Kendall arrived in the world demanding her own way. No, she would not go to sleep in her own crib. No, she would not eat green beans, play in the playpen, or tolerate water in her bottle.

Her strong will, now properly channeled, serves her well as a young woman. It has enabled her to become an excellent gymnast. Because her resolve is strong, she trains hard, refusing to allow tired muscles to interrupt her regimen. She is also a fine student because her steely determination helps her push through the barriers to her goals. And she is a natural leader because she is far more directed by her own agenda than by peer pressure.

In the midst of the power-struggle years, my husband and I weren't always able to see the upside of raising a strong-willed child. There were many scenes that we look back on and laugh about... now. At the time, we were exasperated beyond belief. One memory of Kendall that stands out is of our second summer vacation with

her. Just over a year old, she was barely walking and was an absolute delight 90 percent of the time. She was a busy baby, and so
we traveled with as many distractions as a Honda Civic could hold.
We tied a variety of treats and toys to her car seat so we could travel
decent distances between her protests. In spite of our creativity and
forethought, the trip quickly became a parenting nightmare. Kendall's protests were frequent, loud, and angry.

We survived the trip *to* the cottage, but decided we could not
face the return trip without a new, stronger intervention. We gave
her nausea medicine that tends to make children sleepy. Now I can
imagine some child advocates rising up with indignation to deliver
long speeches about the detrimental effects of medication on children. They have a point! I'm not proud of giving my child motion
sickness medicine in the hope that it would help her sleep. But I'm
willing to bet that if you'd been in the car with us, you would have
considered the same thing. Maybe you have even done the same
thing or wanted to.

It was supposed to work like this: We would administer the
medicine, and she would drift off to sleep, allowing my husband
and me hours of peaceful conversation as we enjoyed the passing
landscape. Once safely home, her long eyelashes would flutter only
briefly as we lifted her from her car seat and gently placed her into
her crib, where she would sleep through the night.

In reality, this medicine had an odd, reverse effect on Kendall,
rendering her unbelievably hyperactive and unwilling or unable
to sleep. She wailed and raged almost the whole way home. The
farther we got from the cottage, the more tired she became, but she
refused to go to sleep. By hour six of this incessant screaming, my
husband was seriously considering attaching her to the bike rack on
the back of the car with bungee cords just to make the noise stop.
By hour seven, he was demanding drugs.

About an hour away from home, all three of us were a mess.
Every nerve ending in our bodies was standing at attention. And
still Kendall shrieked on. I finally climbed into the backseat, took

her out of her car seat, and held her in a vise-grip. She struggled and fought against me, but I would not let her move. Eventually she wore herself out. Ten minutes from home, she finally fell asleep in my arms.

Okay, apparently Kendall didn't want to sleep. I doubt if she knew why, but she didn't want to. But most of all, she wanted to win. We knew she needed to sleep. The trip would have been so much better for us all if she had, especially for her. But children are not typically great at knowing what's good for them. They just don't know enough.

Who Is in Control?

Does any of this sound familiar? It should because we adults are much the same. We fight to maintain control over people and circumstances and the future. We use our wills to try to sculpt the world to our liking. But in due course, we find the struggle has been futile. We are not in control. The control we had or *thought* we had was nothing but a mirage. We can't hold a marriage together by the force of our wills. We can't prevent the death of a loved one or the loss of a job. We can't hold back the rain or even the tears. We can't make our children obey us, our bosses promote us, or our husbands love us. We are not in control.

So who is?

There is a great deal of evidence in nature to suggest that God is in control. Whether you accept the concept of biblical creation or not, there is much that lacks plausible explanation without the premise of an intentional, intelligent, and interested designer. An example of this evidence that has always amazed me is the way a mother's milk, made from whatever she chooses to eat, is mysteriously converted into exactly the form of nutrition a baby needs at every stage of his development. On the baby's first day of life, his mother's milk contains colostrum, a highly nutritious serum he needs after the trauma of birth to boost his immune system and give him the energy to carry him through his first unsettling days of life outside the womb. But one week later, the milk's formulation has changed to match the growing baby's nutritional needs. The mother's milk will continue to adjust in both quality and quantity to suit the child's changing requirements.

Amazing!

Equally amazing are the forces and particles that comprise matter. Now I am no scientist, and the very idea that I am going to give a brief physics lesson would send poor Dr. Smith, my high school physics teacher, into fits of laughter or possibly give him a stroke. However, here it is. The atoms that whirr around us and inside us and constitute everything we see and much that we can't, are made up of particles. Many of these contain opposing electrical charges. No one really knows why they don't fly apart. Scientists have theories about the strategic placement of neutrons and such, but no one can conclusively explain how these opposing particles that spin around with lots of space between them are held together. Physicists do know that whatever that force is, it is extremely powerful. The force is often referred to in the scientific community as "Atomic Glue."

The apostle Paul, who lived long before anyone even knew what an atom was, unknowingly offered an answer:

> Christ is the one through whom God created everything in heaven and earth. He made the things we can see and the things we can't see—kings, kingdoms, rulers, and authorities. Everything has been created through him and for him. He existed before everything else began, *and he holds all creation together"* (Colossians 1:16-17).

Again amazing!

Maybe Atomic Glue is some of our best evidence that God is in control. Matter holds together, your heart continues to beat, and gravity continues to hold you to the earth where you belong because Jesus wants it to. The universe, and all life in it, is sustained by Jesus' active will.

In light of this reality, what if there is a God who is all-wise and all-powerful, who knows us intimately and loves us passionately? And what if his every action toward us is an expression of perfect love? We would never have to question his motives or his capabilities or his commitment to us. *Wouldn't that be amazing?*

What would life be like if we rested in the knowledge that whatever comes into our lives is allowed by God? And that in those times when he allows the unthinkable, we can know with absolute certainty that he's still on our side and that he will lend us his strength so we can walk through the storm? We wouldn't have to struggle for control when life seems out of whack. We could relax in the embrace of a compassionate Parent who gladly takes the weight of maintaining control off our fragile shoulders. Isn't this an incredible thought?

A Case in Point

Donna Staddon is one of the seven mothers who lost a child in an avalanche tragedy in the Canadian Rockies in February 2003. She described in an e-mail to me what it's like to rest in just such a God when life takes a very bad turn:

> Over the past 15 months there have been many times when I have felt overwhelmed with the loss of Marissa. One of those moments happened last August when Brittany was at camp, and I was at home alone. I had decided to go through a file of receipts. It was full of purchases for Marissa when she started at Strathcona. She had just come back from her mission trip to Mexico. There was a new maturity about her, realizing just what a fortunate life she lived. When it came time to purchase her school uniform and all the accoutrements, she was worried I was going a bit overboard. "It's just too much, Mom," she said. I can remember making those purchases with her like it was yesterday.
>
> So, there, by myself, with a box of receipts, I wept and

I groaned with more pain than I had ever experienced before. Since her death, this was the first time I allowed the emotion to come from way down deep inside and just pour out. I cried to God to hold me and help me through this pain and anguish— I knew he understood the immensity of this loss—he lost his Son— and I depended fully on him to guide me through these difficult times. I felt God's arms just holding me and comforting me. I felt assured that my reality of now wasn't a forever thing. I would see her in heaven one day and that would be for eternity!

> *I will always have times when grief hits me like a wave. I allow myself to have those moments. I will journey through them holding God's hand.*

I have found that this tragedy has brought me so much closer to God. My faith has become stronger, and I have such a deep desire to learn more about God and his Word. I have a clearer understanding of God as my comforter and my refuge. I have seen evidence of his working out details far beyond what I could have ever imagined and have experienced his care for me through the deep, difficult days—which are still happening. I think I will always have those times when my grief hits me like a wave. I do allow myself to have those moments. I don't try to resist or deny them. I will journey through them holding God's hand....

After I expressed this thought to a friend she showed me the Bible verse in Isaiah where God says, "I am holding you by your right hand. I...the LORD your God, and I say to you, 'do not be afraid, I am here to help you.'" I have experienced that, and I have hope. I have often said I wish so much that I was at the point where I am today in my faith journey without having gone through this tragedy. I have learned depths of spiritual truths having come through this. I believe that God is in control today just as he was on February 1, 2003. I believe that God's plan for Marissa's life was to be just as she was—vibrant, living faithfully, impacting others. I do not understand the why of this accident, but because of my deep faith in him, I trust and accept his will in this accident. I am determined to continue on, grow through this, learn from it, and hopefully I will be able to reach out and help others in new ways.

A Bird's-Eye View

We can walk through the peaks and valleys of life holding the hand of a Father God who loves us, is committed to us, and is in control. We experience life like someone watching a parade. We see one event at a time with no idea of what is coming around the bend. God sees the parade from the perspective of a bird soaring overhead. He sees the whole of our lives—and the whole of eternity—all at once. He is in a much better position to judge what is best for you and for me. And he made us this promise through the apostle Paul: "And we know that God causes everything to work together for the good of those who love God and are called according to his purpose for them" (Romans 8:28).

Does that mean good people always succeed and bad guys always get their just desserts in the end? You and I know that life isn't that way—at least not the dimension of life we find ourselves in presently. But for those who choose to live in relationship with God, who love him and live in harmony with his design as it is made known in the Bible, it means that God will never let us down. That he is in control of the events that touch us. When evil interrupts life and steals what is most precious to us, we can know that

God will use even that to our advantage. He will not waste our pain but will use it to draw us to our destiny, to our place of highest fulfillment. But God makes this promise only to those who return his love and are "called according to his purpose for them." That means they have surrendered control to God and welcome his plan for their lives.

God can handle our questions. All of them. He won't become offended or defensive.

Acknowledging that God is in control lifts a huge burden from our shoulders, but for some people it creates a new problem. The admission of God's sovereignty raises questions about why God allows what he allows. These questions are troubling. There is no doubt about it. How can God allow sexual abuse, AIDS, or the death of a beautiful, vibrant teenager in an avalanche? There are times when we have no explanations for what God allows or prevents.

The Twin Towers crashed down on Manhattan, and then out of the dust and ashes of this enormous tragedy rise hundreds of personal stories of God's miraculous intervention on behalf of individuals. Why? Why not just prevent the whole thing? Eliminate the terrorists and the need to intervene on behalf of the few?

God doesn't feel compelled to explain himself to us. But he's not like we are. I remember feeling so worn out by the constant questions of my youngest daughter, Kevann, when she was three or four years old. She was so curious about how and why the world works. "Mommy, why isn't Daddy a girl?" "Well, because God wanted Daddy to be a man." "But why?" "Well, so he could be your daddy." "Why couldn't he be my daddy if he was a girl?" After the fourteenth, "But why, Mommy?" I would sometimes make a rule that I would only answer three "why" questions in a row just to preserve my sanity.

Later there were the times when she questioned my decisions. I tried not to do it often, but I remember moments of becoming weary enough of the argument that I'd end the discussion by saying those predictable words we all swore we'd never say: "Because I'm your mother!" Explaining my reasoning to a child, even if I had unlimited energy, wouldn't have solved the issue because Kevann lacked the maturity to understand my logic.

According to the Bible, God is without limitations. He has no three-question limit. He can handle our questions. All of them. They don't wear him out. He won't become offended or defensive. But he also can't be coerced into answering them, for reasons he keeps to himself. Maybe it's because we lack the ability to comprehend the wisdom of his actions? Maybe he just wants us to trust him the way we want our children to trust us when we make decisions for them that they believe are unfair or that they fail to understand?

The Bible tells the story of a man named Job. If Job were alive today, he would be on the *Forbes* most money list, right up there with Bill Gates. Job had everything: relationships, health, money, real estate, livestock. It's hard to imagine there was anything he lacked. And then he lost it. All of it. Everything but his life. And he suffered terribly physically too. His suffering went on and on, and Job had a lot of time to formulate questions he wanted to ask God about the tragic turn his life had taken. But heaven was silent, and Job could only speculate at the reasons God would allow this conveyer belt of misfortune to keep coming at him, dumping heartache after heartache at his feet.

When God did finally speak, he didn't answer a single one of Job's questions. Instead, God helped Job see the majestic, untainted goodness of who God is. Suddenly, from this new perspective, Job's questions seemed irrelevant. In fact, Job apologized to God for even asking them.

Having answers to the "why" questions of life becomes a lot less important to us when we know the answer to the "who" question.

Who is in control, and what kind of a God is he? What are his intentions toward us?

Colossians 1:15 tells us that Jesus Christ is the visible image of the invisible God. So if we want to know what God is like, we can look at the life of Jesus. Go ahead and take a look. He can stand up to the most intense scrutiny. Spend a few hours reading his biographies found in the first four books of the New Testament. Then tell me whom you have met in your entire life who is more worthy of your trust.

The Good Shepherd is a moving metaphor often used by Jesus to describe himself, according to John's biography of Jesus.

> I am the good shepherd. The good shepherd lays down his life for the sheep. A hired hand will run when he sees a wolf coming. He will leave the sheep because they aren't his and he isn't their shepherd. And so the wolf attacks them and scatters the flock. The hired hand runs away because he is merely hired and has no real concern for the sheep. "I am the good shepherd; I know my own sheep, and they know me, just as my Father knows me and I know the Father. And I lay down my life for the sheep (John 10:11-15).

Now, I am no shepherd and I don't know much about sheep. I do, however, have a little dog. He is one of those new designer breeds. You know, the kind that used to be called a mutt. We call him a Pomawawanese because he is a cross between a Pomeranian/Pekinese and a long-haired Chihuahua. He is a very small dog with big hair and a big attitude so we call him Samson.

I concede it's ridiculous how much I love that little dog. I love the way he welcomes me home. It doesn't matter if I've been gone 15 days or 15 minutes. He's so glad to see me he breaks into a little happy dance. I love that he is my bed buddy. My husband travels a lot, and Samson knows that when Randy is gone, it's his job to keep me company. Instead of sleeping at the foot of the bed where he normally sleeps, he lays in Randy's spot with his head on the pillow.

It's amazing how much tenderness I feel toward him. How protective I am of him. Once while out walking, Samson and I were charged by a Bull Mastiff. I know what you're *not* supposed to do in this situation: intervene on behalf of your own dog because the larger dog may turn on you. But you know what I did, don't you? I didn't even think about it. I scooped Samson up in my arms and pushed my way to a tree. I stood as close to the tree as I could with Samson cradled in my arms and my back to the larger, aggressive dog. The Mastiff stood with his front paws on my shoulders, his jaws snapping only inches from my tiny dog. Finally the brute's owner showed up and called him off.

If you've ever experienced loving a little creature like I do Samson, you know the intense emotions connected to this scripture where Jesus calls himself the Good Shepherd who lays his life down for the sheep. For many people, the image of Jesus cradling a lamb in his arms is extremely powerful.

I know a woman named Lois who first became aware of God's love when she was a little girl and saw an image of Jesus holding a baby lamb. She was deeply touched by the tenderness he portrayed in that picture. She imagined the love Jesus must have for that little lamb and what it would be like to be loved like that. You see, she was living in an abusive home and had never been loved. But looking at that picture enabled her to imagine being in Jesus' arms. In a simple prayer, she placed her life in his hands and accepted him as her protector and caregiver that day. She also prayed that someday God would give her someone to hold her like that and love her like Jesus did that lamb.

Lois lived her life fully. She became highly educated and eventually moved to Brazil. For several years she worked for a non-government organization before returning to the United States to obtain a doctorate degree. With that achievement under her belt, she joined the faculty at a university in Illinois.

Now, let me backtrack a bit. Many years earlier, my Dad's sister, Eileen, married a brilliant man. He was a nuclear physicist—a bona fide rocket scientist who, over the course of his career, taught at several universities, mainly in Brazil. He was everything you imagine an absentminded professor to be. If you're envisioning Dr. Emmet Brown from the movie *Back to the Future,* you've got the right idea. After my aunt and uncle's children were grown, my aunt died of cancer. My uncle grieved deeply but didn't wait very long before beginning an online romance with another professor living in the United States.

They became engaged online. My dad said, "She really should see him first!" But apparently that's not how intellectuals do it. The two professors decided that on their first meeting they would greet each other in the traditional Brazilian way, with a hug and a kiss on each cheek. But when my brainiac uncle saw his little lamb at the airport, he dropped his briefcase and swept her into his arms.

Yes, the woman was Lois! She and my uncle married and lived happily together in Brazil until his death a few years ago. Lois waited a long time for her prayer to be answered—she was 65 when it finally happened! She shared this story about Jesus and the lamb and her prayer at her wedding reception. Over the years God had proven himself worthy of her trust.

Envisioning Jesus, the Good Shepherd, helps us trust God more thoroughly. I believe he gave us this picture to help us know he will protect us from danger, comfort us in crisis, and cradle us in his arms. Understanding the dual truths of God's care and control encourages us to place our lives in his loving hands.

We don't like the idea of surrendering control to anyone. It's scary. It makes us feel weak and vulnerable. But to surrender to a God of love, to the God described in the Bible, leaves us feeling safe and protected, loved and cherished, confident and secure. Living any other way is futile. Any control we think we have is false. The Bible says in Psalm 127:1-2:

Unless the LORD builds a house,
  the work of the builders is useless.

Unless the LORD protects a city,
  guarding it with sentries will do no good.

It is useless for you to work so hard
  from early morning until late at night, anxiously
    working for food to eat;
  for God gives rest to his loved ones.

God wants us to stop our striving for control. He wants us to rest in the security of his care. In Psalm 121:3-4 we read, "He will not let you stumble and fall; the one who watches over you will not sleep. Indeed, he who watches over Israel never tires and never sleeps."

It seems only reasonable that we stop letting all this responsibility we've needlessly assumed keep us up nights. God's up anyway. He is in control. Let him handle everything. Conceding control of the events in your world as they unfold will replace your worry with faith, your struggle with peace, and your grief with hope.

— *Conceding Control* —

1. What areas of your life do you most feel the need to control?

2. Is there an area of your life where you won the battle for control but lost the war?

3. How does your perception of God affect your desire to be in control?

4. In the face of overwhelming loss, how would your response be similar to or different from Donna Staddon's after the loss of her daughter in the avalanche?

5. Romans 8:28 says, "And we know that God causes everything to work together for the good of those who love God and are called according to his purpose for them." What does this mean to you?

6. How does the idea that "it's not all up to you" make you feel? Why?

7. To what degree are you ready to trust God?

4

live generously

Why are giving people happier?

Have you ever met a stingy person who was truly happy? How about a lavishly generous one who was grumpy? Neither description computes. There is a reason we portray the miserly Scrooge as grouchy and the giving Santa as jolly. We know instinctively that there is something about living generously that gives us joy.

I'm not talking about making the occasional donation to some charity for the sake of a tax advantage. I'm not talking about doing a little bit of volunteer work to get someone off your back. I am talking about giving generously because there is a need and you want to meet it.

My Auntie Inez was the most generous and most joyful person I've ever met. How did she get that way? She spent the early years of her childhood in an orphanage, where she heard the story of God's unrelenting love for her. Her response to that story was to place her life in his hands. She began to attend church and prayer meetings. She prayed soulfully for a family, for a place to belong.

Also attending this church were my great-grandparents, John and Mariah Hannah. Mrs. Hannah came home from prayer meeting one evening and said tearfully to her husband, "I can't stand listening to that child pray for a family anymore. We've got to adopt her!" He agreed. They took her in and loved her and raised her as one of their own, putting her through nurse's training and giving her a beautiful wedding. She, in turn, raised two children who gave their lives to humanitarian work.

When I met Auntie Inez she was a widow, and her grown children lived far away. But was she feeling sorry for herself? No way. She was far too busy investing her life in others. She wasn't a woman of means because, in the words of her late husband, "Inez could hand money out the back door faster than I could bring it in the front door."

> *Being generous gives us joy, and our joy prompts us to be generous. We feel honored to be the cause of another's happiness. The memory of the pleasure we experienced prompts us to give again.*

My mother and her siblings loved to visit Auntie Inez at her home in Arkansas. Her joy was so infectious. On one visit, one of my aunts gave her a sweater. On her next visit she noticed Auntie Inez shivering and suggested she put the sweater on.

"Oh, I'm sorry, dear," Auntie Inez said, "but someone needed it more than I did, so I gave it away."

One time when my parents visited her, my dad decided to enjoy a mild evening on the porch. He went to sit down in a well-worn chair that almost collapsed under him. Concerned for Inez's safety, and no doubt his own, he went out and bought her some new patio furniture.

"Inez," he said, "I am *loaning* you this furniture so you can't give it away. I am coming back here someday, and I want to sit on this furniture the next time I come."

Auntie Inez remembered what it was to have to do without— without her own bed, her own toys, her own family. She also knew what it was like to suddenly have all those things lavished upon her, and she never forgot how that felt either.

What is the link between joyful living and generosity? Being generous gives us joy, and our joy prompts us to be generous. We feel honored to be the cause of another's happiness. The memory of the pleasure we experienced prompts us to give again. But some people have never experienced this cycle. It's hard for many of us to get our heads and hearts into that paradigm. Human nature and our socialization tell us to cling and clutch, to hang on to what is ours and get what belongs to the other guy. Whether it is time, money, status, or recognition, we want to keep what we've got and get more besides.

Living generously is not only countercultural, it is also counter-intuitive. We fear if we give something away we won't have what we need. But in God's economy, the opposite is true because what we need is often not what we think we need. Jesus said:

> If you give, you will receive. Your gift will return to you in full measure, pressed down, shaken together to make room for more, and running over. Whatever measure you use in giving—large or small—it will be used to measure what is given back to you (Luke 6:38).

When I was doing research for writing this chapter, I found very few books on the topic of giving. Apparently people aren't very interested in learning to be generous. Judging from the titles of books out there, they are far more attuned to the idea of getting rich and powerful. There are tons of books on how to get money, status, power, and time. But there aren't too many on giving that same stuff away. Even more interesting to me was that most of the books in my local public library available on giving were written from a Christian perspective...almost like giving is God's idea.

Living generously doesn't come naturally to us. I know I'm not a giving person by nature. To learn to live generously has required a series of stretching experiences. I'll never forget what fun it was not too many years back to play "Ring and Run" at the door of a single mom whom I knew was struggling financially. My own little family was struggling too, but not to the degree of this woman and her children. I put $100 in an envelope, and my daughter Kendall and I attached it to the inside of our "victim's" storm door. Then we rang the doorbell and made for the getaway car. Safely hidden down the street, we giggled like pranksters as our friend opened the door, looked around, opened the envelope, and then really looked around, eyes wide.

The next week when I saw this woman, she told me how she had prayed for financial help. She let me in on the amazing way it came. I could hardly conceal my secret or my joy as she thanked God for his generosity because she didn't know whom else to thank. And in reality she *was* thanking the right person because everything good comes from God, including the ability to share and the prompting to do so. In the words of James the apostle, "Whatever is good and perfect comes to us from God above" (James 1:17).

Did we miss the money? Yes, we did. But I wouldn't have traded our joy or hers for five times the amount we gave her!

My husband, Randy, saw the value of living generously far earlier than I caught on to it. On his way home from a meeting one cold winter evening many years ago, he stopped at a convenience store to buy a slushie drink. (A strange choice on a cold night, I know.) As he parked the car, he noticed what appeared to be a homeless man loitering outside the store. Randy made a mental note to lock the car when he got out. As he entered the store, the man didn't approach him for money because he was busy asking someone else. He must have been successful because a minute later he was in the store buying a cup of coffee, which he loaded with sugar.

Once they were both outside the store again, Randy spoke to the man: "Do you have any food?"

"Yes, but it's all frozen," the man said. "I'm hoping to get into a building like a Laundromat tomorrow for a few hours to thaw it out."

Randy gave him a bit of money to buy food. It was then that he noticed the man's shoes. They were several sizes too small. The man's feet were hanging out the back of the shoes and had crushed the heels down.

"I'm concerned about your feet," Randy said. "They'll freeze if you don't get better shoes."

"I know," the man replied, "but these were the best the Salvation Army had."

"What size do you wear?" Randy asked.

"Size 11."

Randy looked down at his own shoes. His favorite new shoes. His size 11 shoes. He knew what he needed to do. A few minutes later Randy reached our home. Accompanying him, as he entered the house, was the strong smell of liniment. I traced the smell to Randy's feet...or rather the strange old shoes partially covering them. Apparently the homeless man had used deep heating liniment to try to keep his feet warm in the ill-fitting shoes.

Randy told me the story of how he came to be wearing the strange shoes and the big smile. And over the next few weeks, every time he missed his own shoes, the smile returned. Randy kept those old shoes in the garage, where I had quickly banished them, for months. Seeing them reminded him of how they came into his possession, and that memory brought him joy.

What do you think would have enriched Randy's life more? Wearing his favorite shoes or the memory of the shocked delight on the face of the homeless man in finding someone who actually cared about his dismal circumstances? The comfort of those new shoes or the knowledge that, if nothing else, at least the desperate man's feet were protected from the cold? It was a relatively small sacrifice that Randy made, but it changed him forever. It made his heart grow.

Going a Step Further

Giving money or even our possessions is not the only way to live generously. And it can be argued it isn't even the best way. We can also give our time. I'm writing this page beside the Waiprous River deep in the Bow Crow Forest Reserve in the Canadian Rockies. There's no need to change my name to Patty Pinecone. This is not my natural habitat. I am simply here donating a week of my time to clean toilets, showers, and dishes (not necessarily in that order) at a camp for 78 junior high students. This is my sixth summer of volunteering here. But that's nothing really. My friend Gail, or Tornado as she is affectionately known at camp, is serving as our head cook. Over the past 25 years she has given this camp and the young people it serves, 30 weeks of her life. Thirty weeks of 15 hour days. That's 2,730 hours of volunteering, in case you're wondering. Anyone who has been at camp with Gail will tell you that she not only serves the best camp food ever, but she couldn't be more competent or committed if she was being paid the salary of the head chef in a five-star restaurant. And if a five-star restaurant kitchen can be described as hell's kitchen, which Gail's son Sterling, an actual chef, assures me it can, then wherever Gail cooks must be heaven's kitchen. No one I know loves and values people more than our beloved Tornado. The time she gives to the campers and staff of this camp year after year fills both their stomachs and their hearts.

There is joy that comes from giving our time, money, and possessions, but we will experience generosity's greatest rewards only if we give of ourselves. Pat Nixon is the founder of the Mustard Seed Street Ministry in Calgary. Now the CEO of a not-for-profit organization that has an annual budget of almost 8 million dollars and employs 100 people, he was once a street kid with an undiagnosed disability. He had ADHD so severely that even if the disorder had been on anyone's radar screen back then, his disability still would have been off their charts.

His hyperactivity was so bad that his parents often looked for ways to unload him onto others so they could have a brief respite. One time his mother took him to Sunday school. Three of the teachers, little old ladies all, wisely decided that the only way anyone was going to get anything out of the lesson was if one of them took their busy little visitor into a separate room to try to teach him. That way at least they could prevent him from completely hijacking the lesson for the benefit of the other children. Thanks to the kindness of those ladies, when Pat left Sunday school that day he took with him a plaque he had made. He hung it on his bedroom wall where he could see it when lying on his bed. That plaque became a focal point and a source of comfort when he lay there recovering from his daily beatings.

In choosing to give, we demonstrate and reflect God's generous nature.

You see, each afternoon when his dad got home from work, he would call to Pat, who was playing in the back alley behind their house. "Patrick, get in here!" And Pat thought if he could just get into the house and into his room before his dad got his boots off, he might be spared a beating that day. But he never could. He could never quite reach the doorknob before his dad grabbed him from behind.

By the time Pat was 12, his behavior was so disruptive at home and at school that his dad kicked him out. His childhood abruptly over, Pat got into all kinds of trouble out on his own: substance abuse, crime, you name it he did it. Often he was desperate enough to break into a house for a bath or to drink anything that contained alcohol—including what's under the kitchen sink—just to stay high.

In his fifteenth year, Christmas Eve found him alone in the world and without hope. He stood on a bridge spanning the Adams River with the intention of jumping into the frigid waters below, forever numbing the painful rejection he had known almost from the very beginning of his life. Looking down into the icy water, he searched his memory one last time for a reason not to jump.

One reason came. Just one. It was what those dear Sunday school teachers had managed to patiently instill into his distracted and disorganized mind by helping him make a plaque. A plaque that read: The Lord is my shepherd.

That's all. Just that one idea. But it was enough to prevent a tragedy. The gift of patience and kindness by three women several years earlier saved a young man's life. And through him, many hundreds of other lives.

These precious women gave so much more than their time. They could have passed that hour they spent with Pat teaching their regular class, as they had intended when they arrived at the church that day. They could have sent Pat out to the hall or stood him in a corner. That turn of events certainly wouldn't have surprised him. Instead they gave of themselves. And Pat learned from their example. He was recently awarded his country's highest honor for lifetime achievement, the Order of Canada, for his work in social service.

The greatest form of generosity is to give of ourselves.

In his book *The Body,* Chuck Colson tells the story of Bob Pierce, another man who lived his life in service to others. He first founded World Vision and then went on to establish Samaritan's Purse. Toward the end of his life, even after learning he was terminally ill with cancer, and even though he was experiencing severe, chronic pain, Bob could not stop working to relieve the suffering of others in the most poverty-stricken corners of the world.

On one such trip, Bob met a young girl who was also dying of cancer. Her disease was more advanced than his, and he could imagine the intensity of her suffering. But here in this place of destitution there was no medicine to help with the pain. She was a stoic little thing. She didn't complain. But Bob saw the agony in her eyes and his heart broke. He thought of the pain medication in his pocket. There was only enough to last him until he got back to the United States. His own pain was severe enough that he knew he wouldn't be able to sleep without the medication. But then again, neither would she. So he gave it to her. All of it. With joy. Knowing that the relief his action would bring this brave young girl was worth the unrelenting pain it would bring him.

For a few days, maybe for the rest of her life, the girl became the rich American and Bob the impoverished, forgotten one. In choosing to give this extravagant gift, Bob was not only giving of himself, he was demonstrating and reflecting God's generous nature.

The Extravagance of God

When we are living generously, we experience joy because we are fulfilling our destiny. We were created in God's likeness, and it is God's nature to give. The evidence of that is all around us. We don't live in a black-and-white world eating tasteless food in a vacuum of emotion. God has given us turquoise lakes and amber sunsets, fuzzy kittens and crunchy autumn leaves, birdsongs and thunder, sweet cherries and fiery peppers, cool water and warm sun, laughter and human touch.

The extravagance of God is everywhere. His generosity goes far beyond what we see and experience in nature. Jesus said, "For God so loved the world that he gave his only Son, so that everyone who believes in him will not perish but have eternal life" (John 3:16).

Every year when we give gifts to each other at Christmas we are, consciously or not, reenacting God's extreme generosity. That first Christmas, God showed us what he's like by giving us his Son. Then, for the next 33 years, that Son, a man named Jesus, continued to express the generous heart of God to his people by healing, feeding, loving, and giving of himself in the most extraordinary ways recorded in history. His final act of love on this earth was giving his own life in exchange for ours to pay the debt of sin we have all incurred against God. And then, just as he said would happen, God raised Jesus to life. He walked out of the tomb where he had lain stiff and cold for three days.

To say God is a giver is the understatement of the ages. We can never outgive him, but we can experience some of his divine joy when we live generously.

At great personal sacrifice, Bob Pierce offered a solution to a desperate need a dying girl could never have met on her own. At great personal sacrifice, Jesus died an agonizing death to give us a way back to God. Something we could never do on our own. The apostle Paul puts it this way in his second letter to the Corinthians: "You know how full of love and kindness our Lord Jesus Christ was. Though he was very rich, yet for your sakes he became poor, so that by his poverty he could make you rich" (8:9).

Jesus didn't just write a check, and he didn't send us a DVD or set up a conference call. He gave himself. He came to us in person. Not in a HazMat suit, impervious to contamination but in the vulnerable, soft, uncalloused skin of a baby. To get a glimmer of what that means, imagine giving up everything you own and everything you know to live with a Stone Age tribe. You arrive with nothing but your birthday suit. No iPod, no TV, no computer, no bank account, stocks, or real estate. No bed, toilet, fridge, or microwave. Nada. Going in, you know you will live among these people for 33 years. Life will be hard from the beginning. You will experience needs of which you have been previously unaware because they have never gone unmet. Life will be hard in ways you have never even imagined, and it will become increasingly unpleasant...until the tribespeople torture you to death.

Is there anything on earth that could make you sign up for such a mission? Jesus did. But his sacrifice was far more extreme. Just as the Stone Age tribespeople would be unable to fathom the comforts you left behind, we can't begin to imagine what Jesus relinquished when he was born on this planet. Having never known anything but perfect love and security, having never been victimized by evil in any form, having never known need of any kind, having always had power over the universe at his disposal, he gave it all up. For you. For me. Out of an outrageously generous heart, he accepted the poverty of earth so that we could one day know the wealth of heaven.

Do you want to get rich quick? Look at the life of Jesus to see how you can emulate the giving nature of God. Jesus never left a place or a relationship having taken more than he gave. He didn't leave this world until he had done what he came to do: give his own life so we could connect with God personally. When we really absorb that, we will live lives that overflow with gratitude and joy. We will exclaim with the apostle Paul, "Thank God for his Son—a gift too wonderful for words!" (2 Corinthians 9:15).

Our uncontainable joy will leave us no choice but to live generously. And if we learn to live like that, we will become rich. We might not have a lot of money, but we will be well on our way to building better lives.

— *Living Generously* —

1. Who is the most generous person you know? Describe this person.

2. What is the link between joy and generosity?

3. What ideas and attitudes keep us from living generously?

4. Have you had an experience in which you gave of yourself but ended up feeling you had received more than you gave? What was that like?

5. What evidence is there to support the belief that God is the ultimate giver?

6. Do you and your family make a correlation between God's gift of his Son, Jesus, and your Christmas gift-giving? How can you make that connection more tangible?

7. In 2 Corinthians 8:9, the apostle Paul says, "You know how full of love and kindness our Lord Jesus Christ was. Though he was very rich, yet for your sakes he became poor, so that by his poverty he could make you rich." How did the poverty of Jesus make humanity rich?

8. How does learning about Jesus' life teach you to live generously?

5

resolve relationships

How can I forgive someone who has gravely wounded me?

Relationships should come with a warning label attached, something like: "Caution: Normal use of this product will result in multiple painful injuries." You don't have to reside on this planet long before getting hurt. I bet most of us don't make it out of the hospital in which we were born before someone unintentionally mistreats us. Thankfully, our functional memories don't go back that far. But we all have scars from childhood experiences: getting chosen last for sport teams; being rejected for not being able to afford the coolest clothes; hearing that we are fat, flat, skinny, or ugly; being verbally or sexually abused.

And that's all before we even make it to puberty. From that wonderful point on, we experience rejection by the only boy we'll ever love, unfair treatment by a boss or professor, not to mention the divorce, the betrayal, the affair, the drunk driver, and so on.

The wounds life inflicts on us are harsh, unjust, and sometimes very difficult to overcome. But while we may not recognize it at the time of the wounding, each injury presents us with choices. We can choose to administer treatment so that the wound heals. We can also make the choice to temporarily anesthetize ourselves with vengeance or to try to ignore the wound even though it throbs painfully and a pool of blood is accumulating around us.

When my husband was a kid, he got a sliver under his thumbnail while on a camping trip. The fact that he still remembers, after all these years, what he refers to as the "Mother of All Slivers" tells you how much it hurt. It throbbed and bled. His parents offered to remove the sliver, assuring him it would hurt less to have it out. But there was no way he was going to let either of them dig under there. He wanted a doctor...and anesthesia.

But out in the wilderness, neither was an option.

His thumb hurt like crazy just to touch it. The thought of someone excavating under there with a needle was almost enough to make him pass out. Days passed and, predictably, his thumb became infected. Now it pounded so painfully he couldn't concentrate on anything else. He couldn't play or engage in his usual activities for fear of bumping it. It wasn't until the pain became unbearable (and his parents found a doctor) that he would allow the sliver to be removed.

Similarly, relational wounds won't heal until we deal with them. Trying to forget about them only causes them to fester and hurt more until, eventually, we become obsessed with the pain. We can't concentrate on anything else. Everything we do is affected by it. Denial is one instinctive response to a wounded heart.

A Tale of Revenge

Another natural response is to lash out and inflict pain on the person who did us harm. This kind of thinking carries with it the immaturity of a "two wrongs make a right" logic, but to our writhing hearts it makes perfect sense. For a while. But the relief revenge brings is, at best, temporary.

Last spring I was preparing to travel to a speaking engagement at a retreat center in the southern part of the province where I live. I had been there before, but being as directionally challenged as I am, I asked Jocelyn, my administrative assistant, to get directions for me. My first mistake was that I didn't specify that she should get directions from the retreat center itself. Instead, she got them from Mapquest. Now Mapquest is usually quite helpful when navigating in an urban setting. But retreat centers are notoriously remote, and this one was no exception. The directions gave very helpful instructions such as "Turn right near three cows and a tree." In no time my friend and I were lost. Lost and late.

Patty, who often travels with me to speaking engagements, was driving my Chevy Avalanche. I, for better or for worse, was navigating. We were trying to find our way back to the main road when out of the ditch, right in front of our vehicle, flew a duck. A large male duck whose navigation system was apparently as faulty as my own. Failing to gain sufficient altitude to clear our oncoming vehicle, the duck collided with the front of the vehicle with a sickening thud. I'm sure he never knew what hit him. We did. And instead of bouncing off the front, he went right through the grill. All of him except his head and his left wing.

If there had been a black box recorder in the vehicle, anyone listening to our reaction would have sworn the truck carried only junior high girls. But before I go further, let me just state for the record that Patty is normally the more levelheaded of the two of us. And neither of us is readily given to hysterics. But at that moment Patty squealed, "I can't deal with this! I can't deal with this! What should we do?" With unusual calm I said, "Keep going. What else can we do?" Then the thought struck us. "What if the duck is still alive?" Another series of squeals ensued.

At this point, we didn't know that the luck challenged mallard had penetrated the grill. And we certainly weren't willing to get out and look. So we kept going. But it was impossible to ignore the duck's head peeking over the hood of the truck and the wing that flapped in the breeze above it. Patty suggested that if we stopped, maybe the duck would slide off the front of the vehicle and we could continue without the constant reminder of the traumatic collision.

We decelerated and slowly the head and wing disappeared below the hood. Greatly relieved, we accelerated again to resume our journey. But once we picked up a bit of speed, the wing fluttered again over the truck's hood. Okay, now we knew we had to get out of the truck and see what we were dealing with. We stopped and walked apprehensively toward the front of the truck. Now it was my turn to freak out. "Gross!" I shrieked. I couldn't even stand to look at the mangled duck and the blizzard of down and feathers plastered to the front of my truck.

In a flash of crystalline clarity, our strategy became clear. We had to find a man. There are times in life when a woman really needs a man, and this was one of them. The problem was that we hadn't seen a single male, apart from the unfortunate duck, for miles. We knew we had to find a town. Towns have men. We traveled in silence for a few minutes, contemplating the unfortunate fate of the duck *and* the truck and tried to ignore the wing in our field of vision. Suddenly it struck me—how it would look to the casual observer to see us driving through town with a duck protruding from the front of our rig. I could imagine the comments: "That's quite a hood ornament you've got there." "That one a'them there Duck's Unlimited trucks?"

I howled with laughter until the tears ran down my face, all the pent up tension of being late and being lost dissipating.

It took two passes through the tiny town before we saw a single person, male or female. Finally we spied a man coming out of an unmarked building. Patty pulled up beside him as he got into his truck. I jumped out and became the damsel in distress. (No acting required.) I said to the man, "I'm hoping you can help us with two things. First, do you know where Southern Alberta Bible Camp is?" He said, "Lady, I just came out of a bar. Do I look like I know where a Bible camp is?" "Okay never mind that," I said. "Can you get the duck out of my grill?" "The what?" He came around and looked at the front of my Avalanche. Well, you'd have thought he was looking at the space shuttle. He thought that was about the coolest thing he had ever seen. He suggested we take pictures of it. I said, "Are you kidding? I can't even look at it, let alone take pictures of it!"

He pulled on some long leather work gloves and extracted the duck by its broken neck. As we pulled back onto the road, he was heading back into the bar to show our grilled duck to his drinking buddies.

When I got back to the city the following Sunday, I was amazed that the headline of the *Calgary Sun* read, "DUCK KILLER." *How did the newspaper find out about our crime?* I wondered. Actually, it was during the NHL Stanley Cup Playoffs, and hockey-crazy Calgary was celebrating our team's defeat of the Anaheim Ducks. It seemed our little incident with the truck and the duck was oddly prophetic. But in a strange twist of fate, the Ducks beat our Calgary Flames and then went on to defeat...wait for it...the Colorado *Avalanche!* In my mind, that defeat will always be a symbolic act of revenge of the duck that lost against *my* Avalanche on that deserted country road. For weeks, even after replacing the grill, we were cleaning down and feathers out of the engine compartment. That unlucky duck was determined to make us pay for what we had done.

Many people take the same approach. They reason that through exacting revenge, the scales of justice can somehow be tipped. If the offender feels worse, maybe the offendees will feel better. But revenge doesn't make us feel better; it only spreads our misery around. It also prolongs it. It's like drinking poison and expecting someone else to die. Only forgiveness truly resolves our bitter feelings.

Deciding to Forgive

Some people think it's the forgiven person who benefits the most when a rift in a relationship is resolved. But in fact, the person who benefits the most is the one who has been wounded. Forgiving stops the bleeding of the hurt person's self-esteem. It closes up the hole in her personhood and prevents the infection of bitterness from setting in. The sooner treatment is administered, the sooner the person begins to heal and can stop being a victim.

If you are alive on this planet, you have been wronged. You have choices to make in connection with those injuries. You can deal with them by forgiving the perpetrators for your own benefit or you can let it slide for a while. But waiting until you feel compassion for the persons who have wronged you—well, that's like waiting until you feel like having someone dig under your thumbnail with a needle. It's not going to happen. Forgive now for your own sake.

In his book *Little House on the Freeway,* Tim Kimmel writes:

> The requirements for maintaining anger and bitterness are steep. You've got to overtax your friendships, ruin special events that could have become great memories, make your kids' lives miserable, get bad reviews at work for allowing your personal life to affect your job performance, prejudge new relationships, isolate yourself from people who need you, and neutralize the impact of God's Word on your life.

> Bitterness affects us physically, too. It might reward us with a miserable night's sleep or an upset stomach. It might spoil our appetite or drive us to eat too much. The relationship between physical health and inner joy is obvious. The unresolved anger and hurt festering in some people's hearts is guaranteeing them a rough ride to the morgue. It also promises to get them there sooner.

Helen and Lionel are dear friends of mine who made a right choice. I have always admired the depth of their humility and faith. But the quality of that was never more evident than after the death of Helen's elderly father. About to celebrate his ninety-first birthday, Helen's dad was in excellent health and living on the land where he had farmed and raised his family. Though he was alone, he was happy and loved to work outside tending his large garden.

Early one July morning in 1996, as Helen's father slept, two young men under the influence of drugs and alcohol trespassed onto the farm and began stealing and destroying everything in sight. Having ransacked the building that housed the farm equipment, they approached the house.

Helen's dad was roused from his sleep by the sound of his door being kicked in. He confronted the boys. The teenagers, concerned that they could now be identified, took the only weapon they had— a hammer—and bludgeoned him to death.

Helen and Lionel took the news hard. Many emotions fought for the upper hand in Helen's heart, but among the strongest was fear. She retreated to her home, withdrawing from her usual activities and friends. The couple installed a security system in their home. They bought cellular phones for everyone in the family. They did anything else they could think of to help Helen feel safe and overcome her fear. But they couldn't stop the terrible nightmares.

> *True forgiveness is the miracle that results when the human will is empowered by divine love. We can't do it on our own.*

In the months that followed, Helen and Lionel spent many hours praying together, bringing their grief, fear, and anger to God. During one of these prayer times, and at precisely the same moment, they looked up at each other and realized the same thing: They needed to forgive the murderers. And what's more, they needed forgiveness themselves for the unkind things they had said and thought about the perpetrators of the crime. These realizations and the determination to act on them set my friends on a journey toward forgiveness and healing.

Later, during the trial, they learned that "John," one of the teenagers, was 15 years old, and the other, "Dave," was 19 years old. The boys were incarcerated in a maximum-security penitentiary in another province, the former to serve a life sentence, the latter to serve several years.

Helen and Lionel began to correspond with the boys, extending and receiving forgiveness. In "Dave's" first letter to the wounded couple, he told them he was a really nice guy and they would like him. Helen thought, *Don't push it,* but the miracle was that they did like him. They even loved him. Helen and Lionel offered to pay for the boys to pursue education by correspondence and anything else they needed to get their lives on the right path.

Eventually they took their friendship to another level and visited the boys in prison. Dave asked if he could call Helen and Lionel Mom and Dad because he had never known his parents. They happily gave their permission, and took this young man into their hearts. And to this day they continue to correspond with "John," who is still in prison.

You may be wondering how in the world this could be possible. Alexander Pope got it right when he said, "To err is human, to forgive divine." That's how. True forgiveness is the miracle that results when the human will is empowered by divine love. We can't do it on our own. We must decide to allow God to fuel our decision to forgive with the love Jesus demonstrated on the cross when, from the vast ocean of his torment, he cried, "Father, forgive these people, because they don't know what they are doing" (Luke 23:34).

The whole point of Jesus' death was to pay for the sins of everyone in the world. Your sin, my sin, and the sins of everyone who has ever hurt us. The Bible tells us in Isaiah 53:4-6:

> It was our weaknesses he carried; it was our sorrows that weighed him down. And we thought his troubles were a punishment from God for his own sins! But he was wounded and crushed for our sins. He was beaten that we might have peace. He was whipped, and we were healed! All of us have strayed away like sheep. We have left God's paths to follow our own. Yet the LORD laid on him the guilt and sins of us all.

This may sound a little strange, but what Jesus' death for us really means came home to me several years ago after I finally broke down and bought some proper workout clothes. It ran against the grain of my natural cheapness to spend money on clothes I was going to purposefully sweat in, but I did so anyway. Two weeks after first using them, I was getting ready to go to the gym, frantically searching in the laundry room for the new shorts and sports bra.

My husband, Randy, asked me what I was looking for. When I told him, he said, "Do you mean the clothes that were in the garbage I took out a couple of days ago?"

It turned out that while I was doing the laundry, the new additions to my exercise wardrobe had dropped unnoticed into the trash container I keep in front of the dryer for the convenient disposal of dryer lint. As the sequence of events leading to their demise became clear, my blood pressure soared, my adrenal glands went into extra production, and my hormones, which in retrospect I realize must have been the main culprit in my overreaction, went on red alert.

It seems incredibly silly now, but I was so angry at my husband. *How could you be so stupid as to throw out new clothes?* I thought... said...well, okay, probably shrieked. Surely after living with me for so many years he would know I never throw anything out. I give stuff away or donate used clothes to a charity, but I never throw them in the garbage. And besides, we work out at the gym together. He knew, or should have known, that those clothes were new. Couldn't he have at least asked me why I'd thrown clothes in the garbage or whether I'd intended to? But no, instead he just carted them out to the street to be dragged off with the week's trash. In that rage-crazed moment, my goal was to make that mistake so painful it would never happen again. Randy was going to pay for his lack of attention, I would see to that.

As I muttered to myself in disgust, however, a light went on in my head. I realized in that moment I didn't have to make Randy pay for his mistake against me. That's not what our relationship was all about. "For better or worse" definitely covered such mistakes as this one. And then another light went on—that Jesus, through his death on the cross, had already paid for my sins and *all* the sins of the world. I realized that whatever wrong is committed against me, whether unintentional or malicious, there is no need to get revenge for it because Jesus has already paid for it. To hold on to it or to try to resolve it myself would only diminish what he has already done.

It's Not Okay

Acknowledging that the offense has been paid in full doesn't mean what happened is okay. Often when I apologize after I've spoken harshly to one of my girls, she says, "It's okay, Mom." And I say, "No, it's not. What I said or did was not okay. It was wrong. But I understand that you are saying you forgive me anyway." Forgiving someone doesn't mean the harm inflicted on you doesn't matter. It matters a great deal. Part of the process of resolving a relationship is owning our injury. It's grieving the loss, the damage, the insult...and then *choosing* to accept Jesus' payment for someone else's sin.

When a person sins, someone always bears the consequences. Let's say your son breaks a lamp running wildly through the house. You may choose to forgive him, but who pays the price? You do. You either live without the lamp or you pay to replace it. If you are out in a social setting and your husband says something that really embarrasses you, who suffers the humiliation? You do, whether you forgive him or not. But in forgiving him, you choose not to hold that event over his head. And you both move on free—you of bitterness; he of guilt.

In forgiving someone, I am letting him (or her) off my hook knowing that God, the only one in a perfect position to judge, has not necessarily let that individual off his hook. The person who has harmed you may be subject to legal action. Forgiveness means that because I know that Jesus has already paid for that sin, I can let the individual who harmed me off my personal hook and hand over to the justice system the responsibility to hold the offender accountable. These are the authorities God has established, and we should employ them when laws have been broken.

I am not saying that we are to become doormats. I don't believe God is asking you to permit someone to habitually sin against you, whether the crime in question is a legal or a moral one. You can put up boundaries to prevent someone from abusing you in the future and, simultaneously, forgive them for past offenses by releasing them from your personal judgment.

It's Your Choice

The journey to forgiveness begins with a choice. Every journey does. I have never suddenly regained consciousness on a plane and thought, *Oh my goodness, I seem to be on a journey. I wonder where I'm headed?* I choose a destination, let's say Hawaii because I live in Canada where it's cold six months of the year, and I can never get too much beach in my life. I book a flight, pack my bags, and head to the airport.

What God requires us to do, he also enables us to do. Forgiveness is powered by divine love. We access that power by accepting God's forgiveness of our own sins.

In resolving a relationship, the destination is forgiveness and the healed emotions that come with it. The decision to forgive is the beginning of the journey. Then other steps need to be taken to follow through with that decision, just like on an actual trip. At any point, the process can be aborted by a refusal to follow through.

I remember being so excited the first time my parents took our family to Hawaii when I was a little girl. Way back then it wasn't easy to get to Hawaii from Calgary. We had to drive 11 hours to Vancouver, take a bus to Seattle, and then fly to Honolulu. The morning of the bus trip, we had to get up very early—something like 4:30 AM to catch the ride to Seattle. If I had been given the choice that cold, dark morning to stay in my warm bed instead of getting ready to board the bus, I would have gone back to sleep. And then about 8 AM I would have hated myself for not making the right choice. Thankfully, my parents didn't leave that decision up to me. But God does leave decisions up to us. He never violates our free will.

Once we choose to embark on the journey to forgiveness, we have to make the choice repeatedly to follow through on that decision to forgive until we arrive at the goal. For most of us, there will be many, many times along the way when we won't feel like forgiving. Times when pain and anger hits us like a tsunami, and we are almost washed away by their intensity. But our will anchors us. Our will is still in control. We still have the choice to do what is difficult in the short term but wonderfully freeing in the long term. And when we reach the end of that road, whether it takes days, weeks, or years, we will know we have arrived. There will be no more pain and no more anger associated with the memories of our wounding. Our heart is healed; our relationship resolved.

How can we find the strength to make the choice to begin this forgiveness journey? Only with God's help. What God requires us to do, he also enables us to do. Forgiveness is powered by divine love. We access that power by accepting God's forgiveness of our own sins.

First John 1:9 says, "But if we confess [admit] our sins to him, he is faithful and just to forgive us and to cleanse us from every wrong." Asking God to forgive us for the ways we've wronged him and others opens the doors to a relationship with him whereby he infuses us with the power to forgive others and live life to the fullest dimension possible.

My friends Helen and Lionel had a choice to make. They easily and very justifiably could have taken their bitterness and rage over the brutal and senseless death of a beloved elderly man to their graves. But if they had, they would have sacrificed their relationships, poisoned their experiences, sabotaged their future, and compromised their joy, all on the altar of vengeance.

Instead they chose life. Understanding that Jesus died paying for their sins too, and drawing on his infinite resources, they chose life and sacrificed vengeance on the altar of forgiveness, mercy, and love.

You can build a better life by resolving your relationships with others. Accepting the forgiveness of God removes the obstacles that prevent a relationship with him, and then you are empowered to forgive others. And extending forgiveness for wrongs committed against you frees you to heal and grow.

— *Resolving Relationships* —

1. Have you ever spent a sleepless night fuming at someone who wronged you? Who suffered more—you or the person who hurt you?

2. In what other ways have you experienced the effects of not forgiving others?

3. How is resolving a relationship problem like removing a sliver? Name all the ways you can think of that forgiveness benefits you.

4. Have you ever regretted forgiving someone? Why or why not?

5. How can you avoid becoming a doormat if you choose to forgive?

6. Do you think Lionel and Helen's choice to forgive was humanly possible? Explain.

7. How does acknowledging Jesus' payment for your sin by dying on the cross enable you to forgive?

8. Is God asking you to decide today to forgive someone? Will you begin the forgiveness journey?

6

accept yourself

*How can I get free of all the lies that have
contributed to my poor self-image?*

In his book *Experiencing Christ Within,* Dwight Edwards tells the
Native American fable of a young brave who found a nest full of
golden eagle eggs. In a boyish prank, he decided to see what would
happen if he put one of the eagle eggs in the nest of some prairie
chickens.

Eventually the egg hatched and the young eagle was raised along
with the family of prairie chickens. Not having any reason to doubt
he was one of them, he emulated their behavior. Instead of flying
and hunting, he scratched and clucked just as prairie chickens do.

Years later the young eagle's attention was drawn to an eagle
soaring overhead. "What a beautiful creature!" the young eagle
exclaimed to his prairie chicken brother, who assured him that no
prairie chicken could ever possibly hunt or fly like this, the most
majestic of birds.

Back to pecking they went. And the young eagle gave up the
fleeting hope that he too could soar.

The golden eagle lived and died knowing nothing beyond the
earthbound life of a prairie chicken.

How far, how fast, how high we fly in life is directly related to
what we believe about ourselves. Those beliefs can be like helium
that lifts us to the heights of our potential or they can be the gravity

that pulls us down to the ground and grinds our faces in the dust. Unfortunately, too often our beliefs are products of damaging messages shot into our hearts like arrows when we were too young and naïve to protect ourselves from their destructive impact.

My friend Monica endured terrible physical, sexual, verbal, and emotional abuse for years at the hands of her grandfather. While he was simultaneously smothering and raping her, he would say, "You're nothing but dung. This is all you're good for." The effects of Monica's abuse have been devastating. She has suffered from sexually transmitted diseases for as far back as she can remember. She has endured seven surgical procedures and many resulting infections trying to correct the damage inflicted on her preadolescent body. But the scarring Monica endured was not limited to her body. The abuse she suffered also mutilated her soul.

> *How many of us never even reach for the noble purposes for which we were made because of what we have accepted as the truth about ourselves?*

Imagine the destructive consequences of those repeated assaults on her personhood at such a tender age. Unfortunately, some of you don't have to imagine it. You've lived it.

Monica grew up to fulfill what she believed was her destiny. Though for many years she had no conscious memory of the abuse in her past, she lived a degrading and promiscuous lifestyle. In the depths of her heart she believed this was all she was good for.

How many of us never even reach for the noble purposes for which we were made because of what we have accepted as the truth about ourselves? We live with many faulty assumptions based on people's treatment of us and conduct the rest of our lives collecting data to support what we already believe. The humiliating comments we heard as children are like tunes we can't get out of our heads. As we mature, others write another verse or two, and we keep them playing. We wear a filter that tints all the scenes of life to the particular shade of self we have assumed, and we become unable to see all the evidence to the contrary. The truth about ourselves, from our very limited and obscured perspective, is a combination of the perceptions of a few influential people in our early life and anyone who subsequently agrees with them. What a terrible way to form a self-image. Yet it's what we do, isn't it?

The Truth About You

Last month I visited a small, traditional Mennonite community called St. Jacobs, in Ontario, Canada. While browsing through an antique store, I came across a needlework sampler stitched with the uneven and unpracticed needle of a young girl. It read:

> The most important
> things in life
> are not things
> done by Sarah
> 1845

There was something about that small piece of stitched burlap with its sad statement that caught my heart. I wondered about the circumstances behind its creation. Perhaps Sarah had done something believed to be arrogant, and the sampler was meant to be a reminder to keep her head down. But maybe Sarah had a spirit and dreams that had outgrown her conservative community. Perhaps she had been assigned the needlework project for the same reason a teacher would make a student write out lines on a blackboard. To drive home the message to conform or "behave." I can imagine young Sarah painstakingly stitching the words on the burlap as their message ground its way deep into her heart: "You are unimportant."

To me that was only the first tragedy.

The second was that the sampler likely hung on a wall somewhere, constantly reminding the young girl to keep her place. *Stay in the background. What you do is not important.* The third tragedy is that someone kept it. Sarah must have grown up. Surely if she had learned to disregard the message memorialized by her own needle she would have discarded the sampler in adulthood. So I wonder... was damage done to Sarah's heart? Were dreams never explored and goals never grasped because of the message on the burlap?

The power of what we believe about ourselves, positively or negatively, is profoundly illustrated by author Frances Hodgson in her book *A Little Princess.* It is the story of a tender, loving father who is raising his young daughter, Sara, alone. They have a special bond. All the nurture and affection the father has invested in his little girl shows in her face, her bearing, and her behavior. All her life she has been told she is a princess, and to her core she believes it is true. Because she knows she is loved, she is loving and kind.

As the story unfolds, the father, Captain Crewe, is called away to war. To provide for Sara's care in his absence, he situates his daughter in a strict New York boarding school for girls of her elevated social station. Sara's father makes sure she has the best of everything, including the best room in the house. Many girls are jealous of her, but her kindness eventually wins most of them over. On her eleventh birthday, news is received that her father is believed to have been killed in battle. Those who resent Sara's inner beauty see an opportunity to destroy it.

The headmistress, a bitter and vindictive woman named Miss Minchin, has resented the privileged young girl from the start. She conspires with the attorney stewarding Captain Crewe's estate to rob Sara of her inheritance. She convinces Sara that she is now penniless, that only Miss Minchin's grudging benevolence will keep her off the street. At this moment of profound grief at losing her only parent, her beloved papa, Sara is also stripped of every vestige of security and she is humiliated.

Having triumphantly delivered the devastating blows, Miss Minchin concludes her callous speech by saying, "I expect you to remember, Sara Crewe, that you're not a princess any longer." Sara's circumstances deteriorate further as the granite-hearted headmistress continues her attempt to break Sara's spirit. She is evicted from her room and forced to live in the drafty, rodent-ridden attic, becoming a servant to earn her keep.

Sara begins to see the discrepancy between her present situation and what she has always accepted as truth. One of the younger girls is curious and hopeful. She asks Sara, "Are you still a princess?" The distraught girl can't bring herself to answer. Still, she knows what she knows. In the 1995 Warner Brother's film version of the story, Sara sits destitute and grieving in her attic room. Miss Minchin confronts her saying haughtily, "Don't tell me you still fancy yourself a princess. Good God, child, look around you. Or better yet, look in the mirror." Yet Sara cannot be dissuaded. She taps into that deep well within, long ago filled by a loving father, and insists, "I am a princess. All girls are, even if they live in tiny old attics. Even if they dress in rags. Even if they aren't pretty, or smart, or young. They're still princesses. Didn't your father ever tell you that? Didn't he?"

> When God sees his precious children discarded as worthless, he is outraged because he knows the truth.

What Sara chose to believe about her identity gave her courage, dignity, and strength even in circumstances that contradicted her worth. The headmistress, on the other hand, betrayed her emaciated self-esteem by the way she chose to demean others, even a grief-stricken little girl, to keep from feeling inferior.

What we believe about ourselves affects the trajectory of our lives, and the jet stream we leave in our wake impacts others.

Imagine a laptop computer being found by a prehistoric tribe somewhere in the Amazon. They have no idea what it is. They have no concept of its value or what it could do for them in terms of education or communication. They try using it as an anchor for their canoe, but it's really not heavy enough so they go back to using a rock. They try using it as a chair, but it's too small and not as comfortable as their pile of soft moss and leaves. Eventually they try using it as a weapon, but it smashes to pieces the first time they club something with it. They conclude it is worthless and abandon it.

From their perspective, their conclusion is logical. Though I will admit I have at times fantasized about clubbing my computer to death, in reality no sane person who understands the value of a personal computer would do such a thing. To us, the very idea is outrageous.

I think that is how God feels when he sees his precious children discarded as worthless. He is outraged because he knows the truth about us. In fact, he not only knows the truth, he *is* the truth. Jesus said, "I am the way, the truth, and the life" (John 14:6). Truth is a person—the person of Jesus Christ. What Jesus said and how he lived his life are the standards by which we should measure all the messages that flood our senses. Truth is not what we needy, messed up, selfish humans think. Not one of us is objective. Only God is. So if we want to have an accurate self-image, we have to know what he says about us. We could spend the whole day exploring that topic, and we'd have only scratched the surface. But let's look at three key indicators of our value to God...and, therefore, of our *true* value.

Indicator 1: *We Are His Masterpieces*

Consider these words from Ephesians: "For we are God's masterpiece. He has created us anew in Christ Jesus, so that we can do the good things he planned for us long ago" (2:10). We weren't created on an assembly line. We are each unique and perfect. All blotches, splotches, and other irregularities are intentional and do not diminish our value. Not only are we one-of-a-kind works of the ultimate artist, but each of us carries a likeness to that artist, to God himself. In Genesis 1:27 we are told that we have been created in God's image. We all reflect to the world some aspect of our Creator. And you thought wearing Tommy Hilfiger or Burberry was cool! As the psalmist puts it:

> You made all the delicate, inner parts of my body and knit me together in my mother's womb. Thank you for making me so wonderfully complex! Your workmanship is marvelous—and how well I know it. You watched me as I was being formed in utter seclusion, as I was woven together in the dark of the womb. You saw me before I was born. Every day of my life was recorded in your book. Every moment was laid out before a single day had passed. How precious are your thoughts about me, O God! They are innumerable! (Psalm 139:13-17).

Indicator 2: *He Created Us with the Dignity of Free Will*

We are not robot beings who have no choice but to serve God. He didn't want the subservience of slaves but the love of children, even knowing that we would all—every last one of us—choose in our own way to live independently of him. Nevertheless, having taken the risk of losing our love, he wasn't willing for us to be lost to himself forever. So in the most extreme, radical rescue mission ever launched, he asked his son to be a sacrifice to pay for our sins to make reconciliation with him possible.

Still, having forfeited so much, he leaves us with the dignity of choice. As John 3:16 puts it: "For God so loved the world that he gave his only Son, so that everyone who believes in him will not perish but have eternal life."

Indicator 3: *God Paid Dearly for the Possibility of Relationship with Us*

One indication of a commodity's value is the measure of what someone is willing to pay for it. God was born on earth in the form of the baby Jesus to die for us. God came with skin on in the wild hope that each of us would respond to his love and not reject him. Listen to the apostle Peter:

> For you know that God paid a ransom to save you from the empty life you inherited from your ancestors. And the ransom he paid was not mere gold or silver. He paid for you with the precious lifeblood of Christ, the sinless, spotless Lamb of God. God chose him for this purpose long before the world began, but now in these final days, he was sent to the earth for all to see. And he did this for you (1 Peter 1:18-20).

We can know all about our value to God on an intellectual level, but if we have spent our lives immersed in deception about our actual worth, we may have trouble accepting the truth. I know an elderly woman named Jean who has lived a tragic life. She needs a heavenly Father to run to. She even longs for him. But she is convinced it is too late for her because she chose for so long to live without him. She bought into the idea that her poor decisions and failures preclude her from being embraced and accepted by God. She is believing a lie.

There are so many ways the Bible illustrates the loving acceptance we experience from our God. There's Jesus' story of the prodigal son. An ungrateful and rebellious son demands his inheritance early, in effect saying to his father, "I wish you were dead." Then he takes it and squanders it on a destructive lifestyle. He eventually comes home broken and starving with nowhere else to go.

The way the father in the story responds to this son tells us a lot about God the Father. And, of course, that was Jesus' point in telling the story. The father isn't standing at the end of the driveway with arms folded across his chest waiting to deliver a lecture beginning with the words, "I told you so." Instead, he did something unthinkable for an older man of that Middle Eastern, first-century culture. He ran. He hiked up his robes and ran to meet his son because he couldn't get his arms around that boy soon enough. Jesus' words, his teachings, illustrate the truth about our value to him.

But Jesus went much further than that. He demonstrated it even more through his life and his death. There's the way Jesus granted forgiveness and an invitation to heaven to the criminal dying on the cross beside him. The key word here is "dying." The man is on death row. He is in the process of being tortured to death for a life of crime. Crucifixion was reserved for the most heinous criminals...and for Jesus. That Jesus was subjected to such a terrible death implies something astounding: Jesus' death covers the worst of our failures.

When the man on the cross beside Jesus humbly asked for a place in the future God has created for those who love him, there was no longer any opportunity to clean up his act and make amends for a misused or wasted life. There was nothing left for this criminal to do but throw himself on God's mercy, to ask for and receive his acceptance and forgiveness. The amazing thing is that Jesus extended what the thief had no right to ask for. He said, "I assure you, today you will be with me in paradise" (Luke 23:43).

There's also the story—and this is my favorite—of Jesus' close friend and colleague, Simon Peter. We don't have space here to retrace all of Peter's steps, but let's just look at the events in his life in the days surrounding Jesus' death and resurrection:

- ~: "Oh, Lord, I'll never leave you," Peter says. "These guys might, but not me. I'm the rock, remember?"

- ~: An angry mob surrounds them. Whack. In an act of bravado and an effort to protect Jesus, Peter hacks off someone's ear. Jesus says, "Put the sword away." *What? No sword?* Peter wonders.

- ~: Guards lead Jesus away, and Peter, his courage evaporating, follows at a distance.

- ~: Someone recognizes Peter as a student of Jesus: "Hey, you were with Jesus."

~: "I don't know what you're talking about," Peter answers.
(That's denial number one.)

~: "This man was with Jesus."

~: "I do not know the man." (Denial number two.)

~: "You must be one of them; your accent gives you away."

~: More emphatically now: "I don't know the man."
(Denial number three.)

~: A rooster crows announcing the awakening day. Immediately Peter remembers Jesus' words sadly spoken only
hours ago: "Before the rooster crows tomorrow morning,
you will deny me three times" (Luke 22:61).

~: Weeping...regret...remorse...hiding.

How does Jesus respond to a failure like Peter? He instructs the
angel to tell the women at the tomb on the morning of his resurrection to go tell *Peter* and the other disciples that he's alive. I find
it intriguing that it wasn't John who was singled out. It wasn't the
success story, the only disciple who didn't run and hide. It was Peter,
the biggest failure in a group of failures. As told at the end of the
Gospel of John, Jesus, in a spirit of tenderness and understanding,
later gives Peter the opportunity to affirm his love for him three
times, as if to cancel out the three times Peter denied even knowing
him, restoring his position of leadership among his peers.

Experiencing Jesus' love, acceptance, and forgiveness—seeing
himself through Jesus' eyes—ignited a serious change in Peter.
Instead of living the life of a cowardly, conceited wannabe, he began
to live his true destiny as a fearless child of God. He preached to
thousands, even while under government threats. He stood up to
those who had masterminded Jesus' murder. He endured repeated
assaults and imprisonment. And ultimately, according to tradition,
Peter chose to be crucified upside down because he wasn't willing to
be afforded the honor of dying the same way as his Lord.

Choose to Soar!

Seeing ourselves through Jesus' eyes changes us just like it changed Peter. When we draw deep into that well of worth our Creator and Father has placed inside of us, we find the courage, strength, and dignity to become all he created us to be. Grasping the truth of who we are defines our destiny. When we believe we are prairie chickens, we scratch for what we can get. But when we know we are eagles, we soar!

My friend Monica, so cruelly abused in her childhood, knows her true identity now. She has experienced the radical love, acceptance, forgiveness, and healing of Jesus in her life. Today she is living out her true destiny. Not as dung, only good for one thing, but as a radiant daughter of God, fulfilling her purpose in this world as a compassionate, confident, creative woman. The kind of woman who lights up a room.

Who are you? Have you accepted the opinion of someone who knows nothing about the true you? Has the glorious truth of your identity begun to dawn on you? I hope so. What you believe about yourself radically affects the way you live your life: the goals you reach for, the heights of character you aspire to, the way you relate to people, the way you connect to your Creator and Father. Believing the *truth* about your identity—that you are a valued creation—enables you to build a fulfilling life.

— *Accepting Yourself* —

1. Who were the people in your early life who most formed the development of your self-concept? Were they right about you?

2. What lies have you believed about yourself?

3. Have your misbeliefs prevented you from reaching your potential? How?

4. "Truth is a person, the person of Jesus Christ. Truth is not what we needy, messed up, selfish humans think. Not one of us is objective. Only God is. So if we want to have an accurate self-image, we have to know what he says about us." What is your response to these statements?

5. What three reasons do we have for knowing we are valuable to God?

6. What did the apostle Peter do that left him feeling unworthy of God's love?

7. What did Jesus do to change his mind?

8. How is what you are learning changing the way you think and feel about yourself?

7

conquer discontentment

How can I appreciate what I have instead of making myself miserable trying to keep up with the Joneses?

A woman went shopping for a husband at New York City's famous Husband Store. The rules for the store, posted in the lobby, announced that a person could only shop at the store one time. She could choose a man from any of the six floors of the store, but once she left a floor, she couldn't return to it.

The woman begins on the first floor where the signage read, "These men have jobs."

Employment is a good feature, she thought, but she was pretty sure she could do better. She rode the escalator up to the second floor and read the sign that said, "These men have jobs and love kids."

That's not bad, she thought, but wondered what was further up. The sign on the next floor read, "These men have jobs, love kids, and are very good-looking."

The woman was very tempted but could hardly wait to see what was waiting upstairs. She rode the escalator on up.

The fourth floor had a sign that said, "These men have jobs, love kids, are very good-looking, and extremely romantic."

The woman could hardly contain her excitement and thought, *If this is what's on the fourth floor, I can only imagine what is further up!* She didn't have to wait long because she quickly moved to the next level. There the sign said, "These men have jobs, love kids, are very good-looking, are extremely romantic, and do housework."

"Oh, mercy!" she says. "If these men are so nearly perfect, what is on the sixth floor?" Though sorely tempted to choose a *near perfect* man, her curiosity gets the best of her and she continues up to the final floor.

On the top floor the sign read, "There are no men on this floor. It exists merely to point out that women are never satisfied."

The Plague of Discontent

Yes, almost all women struggle to some degree with discontentment. For some of us, however, discontent is like a wet blanket that covers most of our lives. For instance, most of us are unhappy with our bodies. The 2005 Dove Global Study indicates that 90 percent of women aged 15 to 64 worldwide want to change at least one aspect of their physical appearance, with body weight ranking the highest. Women have been known to try everything from starvation diets to plastic surgery to gain the coveted Barbie-doll shape.

Our life circumstances are another battle zone of discontentment. Women have been known to complain about whatever stage of life they find themselves in. An anonymous writer captured this tendency:

First I was dying to finish high school and start college

And then I was dying to finish college and start
   working

And then I was dying to marry and have children

And then I was dying for my children to grow old
   enough for school so I could return to work

And then I was dying to retire

And now, I am dying...and suddenly I realize I forgot
   to live

Often our dissatisfaction relates to our economic status. We click on our TVs and are inundated with messages telling us what we have is simply not good enough. We need that thingamabob they are selling to be happy. Here are some advertisement slogans I found within a half hour of looking: "Uncover Your Softest Skin." *Oh, no! Maybe my reptilian skin is showing.* "Get Your Zest Back." *Has my zest gone missing again?* "The Hair Color You've Just Got to Have." *My hair really is looking like a dead mouse, isn't it?* "Start the Career You Want Today." *My job is getting so old.* "Get the Gift You Really Want." *I always have to compromise.* "What You Want Is What You Need." *I gotta have it!*

One of the criteria for an effective advertising slogan is that it makes the consumer feel a desire or need. In other words, it intentionally makes us discontent! We feel dissatisfaction when we look around and see women who have nicer clothes and take better vacations and drive more prestigious cars and live in bigger houses.

Early in my career as an interior designer, my husband and I were economically challenged. Randy had recently finished college, and we had just taken a bath on the sale of our first house—a sale prescribed by our move to another city to begin his career. My job entailed spending thousands of other people's dollars to make their homes and commercial properties look fabulous. I came home at the end of the day to our shabby little house and made a mental list of everything I wanted to do to improve it. The list was as long as your arm. Then I would scrimp and scrape and save to gather the money required to buy the first thing on my list. I would also press my somewhat reluctant husband into service because we couldn't afford a contractor or installer.

I quickly discovered something interesting. After we owned or installed the coveted item, I was no more content than I was before. I remembered the grandeur of some of my clients' homes and simply shifted my attention and energy to obtaining the second item on my list. The problem with this approach is that no matter how much we have, there is always someone who has more.

One of my clients was a wealthy woman who owned three modest but inviting and comfortable hotels. I had done work for her in one of the hotels and in one of her three lovely homes. Upon returning from a trip to Las Vegas where she had stayed in one of the strip's opulent new resorts, she confessed to me she wanted to take an ax to the hotels she owned. Discontent isn't restricted to money-challenged people.

The Comparison Trap

Whatever our areas of discontent, I believe the source is the same. It is comparison. Selective comparison, to be exact. For example, my client wasn't comparing her hotels with some rat-infested dive in the red light district of a third world country. She was comparing them to some of the most lavish accommodations in the world. And we don't usually compare our appearance to that of a bag lady. We have our eye on the glossy covers of fashion magazines.

Wayne Rice, in his book *Hot Illustrations for Youth Talks,* tells the story of a photo of the actress Michelle Pfeiffer on the cover of a major women's magazine. Her image was the epitome of feminine beauty. What the average admirer of that flawless face would never have guessed, however, is what it took for Michelle to look that way. Her photo required $1,500 worth of touch-up work, including cleaning up her complexion, softening her eye line, adding color to her lips, trimming her chin, adding forehead (who knew you could have forehead augmentation?), removing her neck lines, adding blush to her cheeks, and adding hair on top of her head...and that's just for starters. Never mind whatever beauty regimen she had been through before the photo was taken.

When I became pregnant with my first child, I was so hungry I ate everything that didn't eat me first. I began to pack on the weight. I didn't really like having extra chins and thunder thighs. I didn't panic, though, because big babies run in my family. My mom had big babies and my sister had recently delivered a whopping 10½ pounder.

When people commented on my weight gain (and weren't they such dears to do so?), I just said, "I'm gonna have a big baby. That's what we do in our family." However, I would glance over at another woman in my circle of acquaintances who was due to have a baby around the same time and notice she didn't have extra chins or thunder thighs. *Oh, well,* I said to myself, reverting to my cover story, *I'm gonna have a big baby.*

I was not surprised when my labor was long and hard. It isn't easy to deliver a big baby, you know. Twenty-three-and-a-half hours after it began, with the assistance of a small army of health-care professionals and the infamous salad spoons, I gave birth to Kendall Hope, who weighed in at an unimpressive 5 pounds, 15 ounces. I was so embarrassed. I thought of the 40 pounds I had gained and said to my doctor, "You better see if there is another one in there because otherwise the rest of this is me."

> *What or who we compare ourselves to is seldom real. We pick one aspect of someone's life that is working really well for her and compare it with an area of our life that is messy.*

Of course the other woman, who was due the same time I was, wore her prepregnancy blue jeans home from the hospital. I couldn't help but compare myself with her. I felt so unattractive. Later I learned what I was comparing myself with wasn't real. She wasn't a healthy pregnant woman. She was a woman with an eating disorder that had threatened her life and the life of her unborn child.

What or who we compare ourselves to is seldom real. We pick one aspect of someone's life that is working really well for her and compare it with an area of our life that is messy. We may feel inferior to a woman who has perfect self-control over her weight, not realizing that every day, behind closed doors, she completely loses her temper with her kids. We may compare our bucket of bolts with another woman's shiny new ride, unaware that she is in debt up to her eyeballs.

You watch your neighbor leave for her prestigious job each day in her cute little suit and high heels while you are searching for your countertop beneath a pile of dirty dishes and wearing baggy sweats that smell like baby barf. What you don't know is that every time she sees you holding your baby, she has an ache in her heart that just won't go away. She would give up all her glamor in a minute if she could have a baby of her own to hold.

Perfection just isn't real.

Your Attitude Makes the Difference

What is real is that we can conquer discontent if we choose to. It isn't about getting the pot of gold at the end of the rainbow; it begins with appreciating the rainbow itself.

I find it so interesting that the Scripture's most direct teaching on contentment, as we will see, begins with these four words: "How grateful I am." These words provide the perspective we need to conquer discontentment. We make the choice daily, hourly, even moment by moment, to gain this perspective by focusing on what is wonderful about our lives instead of what we lack. The glass half-full versus half-empty view.

In Torrington, Alberta, Canada, there is an attraction called the Gopher Hole Museum. It's adorned and watched over by a 12-foot statue of the venerable rodent affectionately named Clem. In an area of the world with nothing but the occasional oil pumpjack to break the monotony of one farmer's field after another, the resourceful, unfailingly optimistic, if not quirky people of Torrington found a way to exact revenge on the furry little pests that have tormented farmers for centuries.

These folks somehow catch, kill (humanely, I'm sure), and stuff their furry little assets. They then dress them in costumes and arrange them in anthropomorphic settings...like a hair salon, for example, which is explained with the caption: "I'm a beautician not a magician!" There is a Royal Canadian Mounted gopher, and what is a Mountie without his faithful mount? (Oddly, also a gopher.) And, of course, a gopher reverend complete with vestments, a pulpit, and a gopher angel hovering overhead.

People come from all over the world to see this museum. What to many would be nothing more than road-kill, the residents of Torrington have turned into a resource. Talk about glass half-full thinking!

I have a friend who has made it a practice (for a period of time) to record in her journal every day—with no repeats—three things for which she is thankful. How long could you go on like that? If one day would be a challenge, you need an extreme makeover of your perspective.

The way we look at the challenges and inconveniences of life are very telling. Sometimes the very thing we complain about is a by-product of having so much. We complain about being so busy but forget that it is because we have meaningful work and relationships. We complain about our mortgage payments but forget that we have them because we are blessed with homes. Personally, I complain about the state of my daughter's room, frequently wondering if she was raised by wolves, but I forget to be thankful she chooses to be at home and not out on the streets running with wolves.

I am annoyed by my husband's loud and erratic snoring and forget to be grateful that I share my bed with a wonderful man who adores me.

I whine about those few extra pounds that keep finding my thighs before I am reminded that my thighs, though not as firm and lean as I would like, enable me to walk and ride a bike and get my sorry carcass to the gym—and that I have plenty to eat.

I complain about the mounds of laundry my family generates instead of thanking God that I have a family, the ability to buy clothes for them, and a washer and dryer instead of a river and a rock.

Now vs. Eternity

Our perspective changes at an even deeper level when we approach the world with the attitude of the apostle Paul. In Philippians 4 he says, "How grateful I am for the concern of my friends..." Then he goes on to speak of the priorities related to conquering discontentment. He makes it pretty clear he has learned to live for the line not the dot. What do I mean?

The Bible teaches that our lifetime is merely a dot on a line that goes on forever. Yet many of us live with priorities that are all about the dot. We say that someone who fails to save for retirement is shortsighted, but what do we do? We live as though this life, this speck on the face of eternity, is the only moment that matters. And then we wonder why we feel unhappy. Ecclesiastes 3:11 states: "God has made everything beautiful for its own time. He has planted eternity in the human heart, but even so, people cannot see the whole scope of God's work from beginning to end."

God has placed eternity in our hearts, and our culture does everything it can to remove it. It is almost successful. One of the ways our culture uproots eternity as though it were a tenacious weed is by tainting our view of heaven. The common conception the average person holds of eternal life is completely unlike what is described in the Bible. We tend to envision a future in heaven filled with chubby, childlike, or effeminate angels strumming golden harps on fluffy clouds while we float disembodied on the breeze or sit through an unending, mind-numbing church service. Others envision eternal life as a whole lot more of the realm we are living in right now. One of my close friends had lived a very hard and painful life prior to finding faith in her late twenties. One day, before Jesus began an extreme makeover of her life and relationships, someone representing a religious group came to her door offering her the opportunity to live forever. She was unimpressed. She said, "Are you kidding? More of this? I just want out of here at the first available opportunity!" Apparently an eternity of the kind of life she was living at that point was not a big selling feature.

Yet there is this nagging discontent that reminds us that our lifetime is too short, our personal stories too small for the eternity in us. According to the Bible, heaven is a place of thrilling adventure, intimate relationships, uncompromised physical bodies, stimulating work, impressive cities, untainted nature, and unbridled pleasure. It's everything good this world has to offer...only a million times better. Life in that dimension will be uncontaminated by evil of any kind. There will be no war, no hunger, no disease, no death, no conflict, no fatigue, and no tears forever and ever and ever and...Well, you get the idea!

That is the eternity God has in store for us. That is the life we were created for. Our longing for life the way it was meant to be is what reminds us that this isn't it. This is just the dot. The only way to address this yearning is to live for the line.

But let's say this is wrong. Let's imagine, for the sake of argument, that there is no line. Life really is all about the dot. Then the yearning in our hearts for something more can never be satisfied, only medicated. So our only hope is to get happy and stay happy because life is short and that's all there is. But getting and staying happy means I will have little patience for anything meaningful that involves delayed gratification. After all, anything that is hard or takes a long time is wasting some of the 80 or so years I get to be happy. For example,

> *We can enjoy the small things in life and be grateful because we know it's a small taste of what eternity holds in store.*

if my marriage isn't making me happy, there's no time to waste in trying to fix it. I should just get a new one. And surely if I were more beautiful I would be happier. Maybe a little nip here, a tuck there. Sure, people say that money can't buy happiness, but no one really believes it. If they did, they wouldn't buy lottery tickets. More money means more stuff. Stuff will make me happy. So the pressure is on to be as beautiful, rich, and important as possible because those are the things that our dot-oriented culture tells us are the paths to happiness.

The problem is that we never reach "enough." Hollywood is full of women who have had so many plastic surgeries they look like actual plastic. Yet there are still people who look younger and/or more beautiful. And no matter how much money or stuff we have, there is always more to be had. Someone else's life always looks more fulfilling, so life becomes an incessant, exhausting game of "Keep Up with the Joneses." And the one who dies with the most toys…well, she still dies.

Where is the contentment in that?

On the other hand, if the Bible is right, if this life really is nothing more than a dot on an eternal line, then a whole new perspective emerges. Since I realize that this life is such a small fraction of what I will ultimately understand and experience life to be, I will invest my life in things that matter now but that will also outlive my 80 years. I will have patience for the things that bring meaning not merely happiness, even if those things take a long time. I am able to enjoy the small things in life and be grateful for whatever good I find in it, realizing that the good I experience here is a small taste of what eternity holds in store for me. I don't dread the end because I know it is really the beginning of a dimension of life in which I will be more alive than ever before.

An Amazing Truth

I traveled to Trinidad with a group of young adults on a short-term mission one December. While working in a makeshift medical clinic in a shantytown called Betham, I met an elderly woman. She "got it." She really knew what it was to live for eternity. She had brought her grandchildren, for whom she was sole provider and guardian, to see the doctor. She had also asked the physician on our team to examine her arthritic hands, which were frozen into gnarled claws. I spoke to her after she was treated. Because she looked so thin and frail, I asked her if she had enough to eat. I will never forget her answer because it broke my heart and rocked my world.

"Sometimes we have enough to eat," she said, "and when we don't, I feed the children what there is, and I make a tea out of lime leaf and orange peel to make the pain in my stomach go away. But I can never complain because Jesus has been so good to me." What broke my heart was that so much of the world has to live like this sweet grandmother. I can picture her cooking over a primitive stove, washing clothes under a pump, and fixing the leaky roof of her little shack—and all with those painful, deformed hands. What rocked my world was that even in these desperate circumstances she was grateful. She was saying with the apostle Paul:

> I have learned how to get along happily whether I have much or little. I know how to live on almost nothing or with everything. I have learned the secret of living in every situation, whether it is with a full stomach or empty, with plenty or little. For I can do everything with the help of Christ who gives me the strength I need (Philippians 4:11-13).

The old woman was saying, "It's not about getting what I want here and now. It's not about the dot. It's about the eternity God has placed in my heart. It's about knowing God, the only one who can fill up the emptiness in me. And by his strength I can handle whatever else comes without losing my joy." That is the power behind conquering discontent. It's God's power. We can't muster it on our own.

Conquering discontent means we learn to appreciate all the good in our lives, realizing its ultimate source. James 1:17 tells us,

"Whatever is good and perfect comes to us from God above." Then we need to live for the line, not the dot, believing that God has placed eternity in our hearts and that the only way to satisfy the longing connected with that reality is to be in relationship with him. From this relationship with God, we will be empowered to conquer discontent and find strength to live with a perspective and priorities that run counter to our culture.

— Conquering Discontentment —

1. In what area of your life do you struggle the most with discontentment?

2. Do you tend to compare yourself with others? What is the outcome of this kind of thinking?

3. List some things you often take for granted but are truly grateful for.

4. What does it mean to "live for the line" instead of the dot?

5. The Bible says in Ecclesiastes 3:11 that God has placed eternity in our hearts. What does that mean to you?

6. What does the apostle Paul say is the secret of being content (Philippians 4:13)?

7. Do you believe a person can be perfectly content without faith in God?

I have the strength to face all conditions by the power that Christ gives me.

8

offload stress

How can I cope with the pressure life
brings and the stress it generates?

There is no such thing as a stress-free life. Whether you are a trauma surgeon or a tree surgeon, stress is unavoidable because it is simply the everyday impact of your relationships and circumstances on your body. Everything you encounter in your daily life has an effect on you, positively or negatively, based on how you perceive and process each situation. Though stress-related factors are responsible for up to 80 percent of all diseases in North America, stress in itself is not necessarily a bad thing. It's how we respond to and manage stress that determines our well-being.

There are certainly lots of things in life we can get stressed about. Huge things happen or could happen to us. We also encounter stress over the daily, little things. When my family was moving back to Calgary several years ago, Randy was unable to clear his schedule in order to house hunt with me. So he stayed in British Columbia with our girls and I went to Calgary alone.

The first day out looking, I found a house I thought was the one. I called Randy, and we decided what we would offer. We placed the offer, the sellers countered, and we prepared a counter to their counter. It happened to be Mother's Day and because their Realtor was unavailable to receive our counteroffer until late afternoon, I took a walk with my sister to try to deal with my stress.

Well, on our walk I happened to see a sign for an open house. We decided to peek inside. I walked in the door. The house was bright and open, and I said to my sister, "This is my house! This is it! It just feels right." The problem was that by this time my Realtor was on his way to present our counteroffer on the other house.

I rushed to find a phone. I reached him just in time. Within a half an hour of my first laying eyes on this new place, there was a sold sign on the front lawn and I had myself a house. All that remained was to tell my husband.

When Randy picked up the phone, I said, "I've got good news, and I've got bad news. The good news is that I bought a house. The bad news is that it's not the house I told you I was going to buy." Then I said, "It's really stressful buying a house alone."

Randy harrumphed and said, "Oh sure, you think you've got stress. I had to do two girls' hair for church this morning."

The Roots of Stress

What stresses you out? Have you ever had one of those days when you're going about 16 different directions at once and nothing turns out right? We live in a culture that is stuck in fast-forward. Our days go by in a blur of carpooling, grocery shopping, working outside the home, working inside the home, volunteering at school and at church, and on and on. There is always far more to do than can reasonably be done by one individual in a day.

Often the stress we encounter is because we are shortsighted. The scene that comes to mind is a quick trip to the grocery store. I don't grab a cart because I only intend to pick up a few things. But as I walk through the store, I keep thinking of more items that I need. Having already exceeded the natural holding capacity of my hands, I struggle to find a way to snag each new article. By the time I make it to the checkout counter, my muscles are in spasms because they have been forced into unnatural hooking, tucking, and balancing positions. Various grocery items are threatening to escape my awkward grasp, and I am seriously wishing I had possessed the foresight to begin with a cart.

We also tend to live as though we have no limits. It's almost as if we think we don't need sleep, recreation, food, or even air. Like jugglers, we take on more and more responsibility without offloading anything. Then we have to move faster and faster to keep all the balls in the air. But accepting our own limitations is crucial to surviving stress. We can't do it all. Each individual has to recognize her own limitations.

I, for example, would be the world's worst air traffic controller because I can really only focus on one thing at a time. Can you picture it? "I know you've been circling the city for half an hour now, but can you come back later? I'm really, really busy now." Or, "I said 7,000 feet? I thought I said 10,000 feet. If you're at 7,000, you'd better move 'cause I'm pretty sure I told the other guy coming toward you 7,000 feet."

We need to give ourselves permission to not do it all.

Some of you can likely talk on the phone, ice a cake, tie a shoe, and change a diaper all at the same time. (Let's hope you can wash your hands in there somewhere too.) If I'm talking on the phone, that's it. That and maybe one more thing if I really concentrate is all I can handle.

And often when we should be resting or sleeping, we are reviewing our impossible to-do list for tomorrow. This is not foreign territory for me, this business of sleepless nights and priorities that keep getting mixed up in an effort to put out the most pressing fire at any given moment. But I'm learning to offload this stress!

Whether we're skilled at multitasking or not, the truth is that we all have limitations. We only have 2 arms and 10 fingers. We only have a fixed amount of time. We only have so much strength. We only have certain talents and abilities. Our brains can only contain a predetermined amount of data before the information starts escaping or becomes irretrievable. We have limits. The sooner we recognize that and prioritize our lives accordingly, the better.

We need to give ourselves permission to *not* do it all. Look around and see the alternative. Women have never been busier or more stressed out. A recent statistic says that two-thirds of married women in the United States who are working outside the home work 65 to 85 hours per week, including their domestic duties. We are told that women today can have it all, but honestly, is this really what we want?

Two Are Better Than One

In this crazy lifestyle symbolized by a clock, a calendar, and a cell phone, Jesus extends an invitation to you and me. He says,

> Come to me, all of you who are weary and carry heavy burdens, and I will give you rest. Take my yoke upon you. Let me teach you, because I am humble and gentle, and you will find rest for your souls. For my yoke fits perfectly, and the burden I give you is light (Matthew 11:28-30).

That's got to be the best offer you've had all day! Maybe your whole life. Rest. Tranquility. Peace. What does this mean? Does it mean we are somehow transported to a beach in the Caribbean without the job, the phone, and the kids? No, it's more permanent than that. The answer is in the part about the yoke: "Take my yoke upon you." For those of you who were not farm girls a hundred years ago, a yoke is the heavy wooden harness that fits over the shoulders of a pair of oxen hitched to a cart or a plow. Now you're thinking, *Oh that sounds restful. I was just thinking the other day, "I'd sure feel better if someone would hitch me up to a plow."*

But don't miss the significance of this invitation. It is an invitation into a relationship. A *partnership* in which we are voluntarily joined to the gentle Jesus by a yoke of love. We were never meant to plow through life alone. We struggle under the weight of our anxiety and stress because we are trying to pull a load meant for two, not one. Jesus, who invites you to share your load, created you. He knows you were not designed to handle all the stresses and worries of life on your own. "Come," he says. "Take my yoke."

Notice that the decision to take the yoke is entirely up to you. No one is going to force it on you, least of all Jesus, who describes himself in this passage as humble and gentle.

A yoke is a symbol of submission and service. At some point yoked oxen surrender their wills, their whole selves, to their master. At first most of us aren't really warm to words like "submission" and "service"—until we realize what Jesus is teaching when he says, "Let me teach you, because I am humble and gentle, and you will find rest for your souls" (Matthew 11:29). Paraphrased, Jesus is saying,

> *When we are in sync with Jesus, allowing him to set the direction and the pace, we never have more than we can manage.*

> I want to free you from people's expectations, the demands of meaningless activity, and your weariness in the search for something in life that really satisfies. I'll show you how to lay down those unnecessary burdens you carry and reorient your life around the good things. I want to teach you how to live dependent on me. I offer you unconditional love...the kind you don't have to perform for. The rest I bring is healing. It results in peace with God. My yoke fits perfectly. I made you, and I custom-made the yoke for you as well. The burdens we will share will be successfully managed if we pull together.

I often think of another example of how we can offload stress. My family does a lot of biking. When my younger daughter, Kevann, was little, my husband pulled her behind his bike in a little trailer. When she got too big for that, we got a Trail-a-Bike for her. You've probably seen one. It's an extension that hitches onto the back of an adult bike. Because this extension has handlebars and pedals, Kevann could learn to balance while being pulled, and she could even contribute to the bike's locomotion by pedaling. On our family bike rides, Kevann could pedal when she wanted to or she could rest and let her daddy do the work when she got tired.

So it is with our lives with Jesus. When we are in sync with him, allowing him to set the direction and the pace, we never have more than we can manage. We can pedal with him, but when the hills become overwhelming, we can rely more and more on him. He offers the strength and the love of a daddy to get us to the top of the hill and over.

Randy and I have a close friend who, in the space of one year, encountered tremendous uninvited and for the most part unavoidable stress. It began with the decision to move his family across the country to be closer to extended family due to his wife's worsening health. After uprooting the family from all that was familiar and starting a new, high-profile job, Brian's wife of 19 years suddenly died. Now Brian was faced with smothering grief, the heartaches of his three teenage boys, single parenting in a new city, and settling into a new job. Within one year, he added another major stressor (although a good one) and remarried.

Though Brian grieved deeply during that year, he never lost his sense of humor. Several times he jokingly mentioned the type of psychological testing that assigns a numeric value to significant life stressors in order to predict stress-related illness. He said he didn't even want to know how high he would score on such a test. Knowing might just finish him off. But recently, six years after that turbulent time in Brian's life, I got psychologist Tim Lowenstein's Life Stress Test and completed it on Brian's behalf. A score of 0 to 149 indicates a low susceptibility to stress-related illness. Scoring 150 to 299 indicates medium susceptibility, and above 300 is the danger zone. Brian's score was 381! Amazingly, Brian didn't get sick.

I am absolutely convinced, and I know Brian agrees, he now

enjoys coasting down the backside of that enormous, overwhelming hill because he knew how to offload his stress on Jesus. Brian never attempted to carry the burdens on his own. He placed himself and his sons in the hands of God and trusted him with each challenging moment, hour, and day. Today Brian is certain the outcome for his whole family would have been very different had he faced that steep incline alone.

I don't know what your hills are. Mine are primarily related to work deadlines and balancing the demands of a husband and children with limited resources of time and energy. Maybe yours are crushing financial pressures, caring for an aging parent, a marriage that's coming unglued, or simply trying to survive the stormy adolescence of a rebellious child.

None of these is too complicated or too big for Jesus, nor do any such circumstances in your life ever catch him by surprise. His invitation to people to come to him with their burdens was spoken 2,000 years ago, but it is still open to you today.

A Successful Strategy

Jesus promises that if you come to him he will give rest to your soul. That means he wants you to experience his peace. Note, though, that there is peace *with* God and the peace *of* God. These are two very different things.

Peace *with* God is the rest that comes when we surrender our wills to him. We say, "I don't want to plow through life alone anymore, God. I'm weary. I'm ready to be yoked to Jesus and to allow him to set the direction and pace for my life." It's acknowledging that I am unable to live a life pleasing to God or satisfying to myself independent of him. It's receiving his unconditional love for me demonstrated by Jesus' death on the cross. It's receiving his forgiveness for my wrongdoing and the peace that comes from beginning again with a clean slate.

The peace *of* God is a sense of supernatural calm and well-being that flies in the face of unpeaceful circumstances. I know it's likely that some of you have come to a place of surrender and have invited Jesus into your lives, thereby becoming yoked to him. You have peace with God. Yet maybe the peace of God escapes you.

I fall into this rut sometimes myself. Let me remind you of God's strategy for experiencing the peace of God as outlined in Philippians 4:6-7:

> Don't worry about anything; instead, pray about every-
> thing. Tell God what you need, and thank him for all
> he has done. If you do this, you will experience God's
> peace, which is far more wonderful than the human
> mind can understand. His peace will guard your hearts
> and minds as you live in Christ Jesus.

In implementing this strategy, you're simply saying to God, "Okay, Lord. I'm not carrying this load by myself anymore. I can't do it. I'm giving this concern over to you. I accept your peace to keep my heart from allowing this particular problem to steal my sleep or my joy from now on." This works. I'm here to tell you that from personal experience.

God's peace is different from what most of us think. It is different from what so many books and systems offer. True peace is not found in positive thinking, the absence of conflict, or in good feelings. It comes from knowing that God is in control and loves us and always acts for our ultimate good. His peace is always available to us. Any time panic or worry overtakes us, we can call out to him in prayer and find rest.

Some of you may simply need to remember to exchange your anxiety for the peace of God. But others of you may not be in a position of relationship with Jesus. True peace isn't available to you because you haven't made your peace with God. Making peace with him is the most profound transaction you will ever make. It's not complex. Let God know your willingness to surrender your will to him. Tell him you're accepting his forgiveness and love and committing to live his way from now on. You do this in a prayer. The exact words aren't important because God knows what is going on in your heart. Just talk to him out loud or silently.

If you invite Jesus into your life, you never need to feel the full weight of the stresses of living in this busy world again. You will have a personal relationship with Jesus that yokes you with him forever, allowing him to share your load. There's no better way to a great life!

— *Offloading Stress* —

1. What are the usual, ongoing stresses in your life?

2. What are some of your recent added or unexpected stress producers?

3. How do you respond to stress? How does your family know you're stressed?

4. What are your usual coping mechanisms?

5. How do you respond to the statement that "Jesus, who invites you to share your load, created you. He knows you were not designed to handle all the stresses and struggles of life on your own"?

6. What is the difference between peace with God and the peace of God?

7. Insert your own concerns into Philippians 4:6-7. Pray it back to God when you need him to help shoulder your load:

> Don't worry about anything; instead, pray about everything. Tell God what you need: _____, and thank him for all he has done: _____. If you do this, you will experience God's peace, which is far more wonderful than the human mind can understand. His peace will guard your hearts and minds as you live in Christ Jesus.

Now claim that peace. Memorize this verse so it is always available in your mind when you encounter stress.

9

plug in

*How can I connect to people and to God so
I am known, loved, and accepted for who I really am?*

A monk joined an order requiring a vow of silence. He was only
allowed to speak every 10 years. After the first decade of his
isolation, his only words were: "Food bad."

Another 10 long years crawled by, and the monk used his rare
opportunity to speak to say: "Bed hard."

After his third decade of silence at the monastery, he said only:
"Room cold."

Soon after that, he left the order. When questioned about the
monk's decision to leave, the head of the monastery said, "Actually,
I'm not surprised. He's done nothing but complain ever since he
got here."

Yes, it's hard to be happy and fulfilled when we're isolated. Some
recent studies support the notion that we are not only happier when
we're plugged in to good relationships, we're also healthier. The
Harvard School of Public Health determined that people with
lots of social connections live longer. In fact, good relationships
were found to be a more accurate predictor of health and longevity
than age, gender, race, or even health-threatening practices such as
smoking, overeating, and alcohol consumption.[1]

Amazingly, scientists have established that people with lots of
relationships are even more resistant than others to the common
cold. Researchers infected 276 people with viruses known to cause

the cold. The people who were well plugged-in socially were four times less likely to be plugged-up nasally. They were also less contagious and produced less mucus.[2] Bluntly stated, people with few relationships are literally snottier!

According to the Bible, God created us for relationship. If that's true, then it stands to reason that the closer we are to him, the more we'll be healthy, content, and satisfied. And the more solid relationships we have with people, the happier we'll be. We all want to be in great relationships. So why is it so hard to find them and then make them work? To understand the problem, we have to go back a long way.

We Need People Too

God created people with the intention of enjoying their friendship. But he didn't want us to be robots or slaves. He craved the love of those who wanted to be his friends, so he gave us the power to choose. Yet even in that perfect relationship between God and the first man, Adam, God recognized that man needed someone like himself and so Eve was created. Adam and Eve lived in perfect contentment, finding their every need met in relationship with God and each other.

There were no arguments or communication problems, no unmet expectations, no jealousy—no relational whitewater at all. Everything was perfect until they decided to exercise their ability to choose not to obey the only restriction God had placed upon them: Do not eat the fruit of the tree of the knowledge of good and evil.

In Bill Cosby's take on the story of Adam and Eve, found in his book *Fatherhood,* God is shocked, after having read his children the riot act about the forbidden fruit, to see them taking an apple break. When he confronts them, Adam tells God that Eve started it. The drama unfolds something like this:

"Did not."

"Did, too."

"Did not."

Having had it with the two of them, God's punishment was that Adam and Eve should have children of their own. Thus the pattern was set, and it has never changed.

If you don't think that's true, then why did that little conversation sound so familiar to you? Because every child born since that exchange in the garden was born with a natural predisposition to do wrong. Sin entered the world the day Adam and Eve defied God. Nothing has been the same since.

What was once a close, personal relationship between the God of the universe and the people he created is now obscured by sin. And this

> *Even though the quality of our relationships changed when sin entered the world, our need for them did not.*

behavior comes naturally to us, but it can't be tolerated by God. Sin has also separated us from other people. Now we preserve extraordinary moments of intimacy in our hearts, not realizing that those few precious times of rare connection with those we love are what God intended to be our normal, everyday experience.

And even though the quality of our relationships changed when sin entered the world, our need for them did not. Though our relationships are often the scenes of terrible crimes committed by us or against us, we continue to need intimacy. So how can we find safe relationships where we can love and be loved, accept others and experience acceptance?

Were you raised in a family where closeness was not valued? You may not be aware of your need for intimate connection. You may not be aware of the various surrogates you have had for meaningful relationships in your life. You could have substituted work, or chat rooms, or romance novels, or many other things for authentic relationships with people in subconscious efforts to guard your heart or mitigate loneliness.

Or have you been badly hurt by someone you trusted? Has it been so long since you've taken the risk of being vulnerable again that you've forgotten how to connect on a deep level? Or do you carry a secret that is connected to so much shame you feel certain you would be rejected if people knew the truth about you? You may have concluded that knowing others and truly being known are not worth the risk of pain. Besides, you're getting along in this world just fine on your own. You don't need anybody. But someone important disagrees with you: God.

> God made our bodies with many parts, and he has put each part just where he wants it. What a strange thing a body would be if it had only one part! Yes, there are many parts, but only one body. The eye can never say to the hand, "I don't need you." The head can't say to the feet, "I don't need you." In fact, some of the parts that seem weakest and least important are really the most necessary (1 Corinthians 12:18-22).

In the Bible, the true church—that is, all Christ's followers worldwide—are described as the body of Christ and Jesus is described as the Head. Obviously a body can't heal or grow or even live without a head. Here's an interesting example of how we need the whole body to grow.

Recently the amazing survival story of Jessica Clement was told on *Oprah*. As a member of the Army reserves, Jessica was deployed to Iraq. On May 5, 2004, she was gravely injured by a roadside bomb. Shrapnel penetrated her lower back and her skull, severely injuring her brain.

Though she was immediately airlifted to Baghdad for surgery, her brain injury was so traumatic that doctors gave her only a two-percent chance of survival. Thankfully the doctor assigned to Jessica's case was neurosurgeon Lieutenant Colonel Jeff Poffenbarger. Before deploying to Iraq, Dr. Poffenbarger decided he wasn't going to give up on anyone. He would do everything that could be done for every soldier he treated, regardless of how slim their chances of survival were.

For Jessica, that meant that he had to remove almost half her skull to accommodate the swelling of her brain. He then inserted the skull fragment into her abdomen right below her ribs to keep the bone alive and protect it in the hope that it could one day be used again to cover and protect her brain. Her body kept that piece of bone alive. Four months later it was reattached to the rest of her skull.

When an organ or bone is removed from the body for transplant, the medical team involved only has a few hours to complete the process before the organ begins to die. Even a sick body is a better storage container for organs and bones than no body. Body parts need a body in order to thrive.

And it's the same spiritually. People need to connect in intimate relationship with God to truly survive and thrive spiritually. They need to be "in the body of Christ," commonly referred to as the church. But one of the consequences of sin was separation between God and the people he created. The only way to reconnect is through a close relationship with Jesus. Oh, you won't drop dead if you aren't in a personal relationship with Jesus, but that part of you created by God for relationship, the real you, will become unhealthy.

Reconnecting

How do we get connected to God and people in a healing, nurturing way? How do we go back to the way it was meant to be? There are two faces to the character of God that we must experience to combat the contamination of sin in our relationships. The two faces are grace and truth. Sometimes we might see these as the good and scary sides of God respectively. But in reality, we have to embrace them both to heal and grow.

Grace is unconditional love and acceptance. In *Changes that Heal*, Henry Cloud defines it as "unbroken, uninterrupted, unearned, accepting relationship." Can you imagine such loving security? It is only when we know our acceptance is certain that we are willing to allow our true selves to be known. Grace is the first necessary element that allows us to risk our vulnerable hearts.

But grace alone isn't enough. We all need that enduring love to outlast the day when the truth about all our selfishness, weaknesses, and failures comes to light. It is only when truth is told that genuine intimacy is possible.

The Bible shares many encounters Jesus had with women. Women who carried around all kinds of shame. Women rejected and ridiculed by everyone but him, who always treated them with kindness and dignity. These women looked into the grace-filled eyes of Jesus and were never the same again.

> *Where do we get the idea that God is always waiting to beat us down, to squash us like a bug? Certainly not from Jesus!*

One such woman was brought before Jesus and the crowd that had gathered to hear him teach. She had been dragged out of someone's bed, having been caught in the act of adultery. She was probably half-naked. I can only imagine her shame as these ultra-religious men stood her before the crowd. Where was her partner in crime? No one knows. Apparently her accusers were only interested in humiliating *her*. Objectifying *her*.

Their righteous indignation at her moral failure was really a ruse to trap Jesus into saying something incriminating. You see, he had a bit of a reputation for showing compassion instead of judgment, and they wanted a legal claim to use against him. To the woman's accusers, she was merely "Exhibit A." But not to Jesus. To Jesus she was first a person—a dear, troubled daughter with hopes and dreams, fears and failures, wounds and weaknesses.

In John 8:3-11 we read her story. The religious leaders addressed Jesus: "Teacher...this woman was caught in the very act of adultery. The law of Moses says to stone her. What do you say?"

Jesus didn't answer immediately. Instead, he stooped down and started writing in the dust with his finger. I would love to know what he wrote. Maybe it was a list of the hypocrisies of the woman's accusers? Maybe it was the *other* nine commandments? We'll never know; the Bibles doesn't tell us. But pressed for an answer, Jesus finally said, "All right, stone her. But let those who have never sinned throw the first stones!"

Back to writing in the dirt he went, and as he did, the woman's accusers slipped away one by one. When he stood up again, only the woman stood where her prosecutors had been. Jesus asked her, "Where are your accusers? Didn't even one of them condemn you?" I can imagine the humiliated woman struggling to raise her eyes to look into Jesus' face. What would she find there? Kindness? Judgment? Hope overcomes her trepidation, and she risks locking eyes with him.

"No, Lord," she replies.

And Jesus says, "Neither do I. Go and sin no more."

Where do we get the idea that God is always waiting to beat us down, to squash us like a bug? Maybe from the religious establishment, but certainly not from Jesus. Jesus didn't gloss over the woman's immoral behavior or pretend it didn't matter, but he didn't condemn her because of it. His acceptance of women like this one must have been all the more precious to them because his grace was bathed in truth. He was not naïve. He knew each one's past. He knew each one's mistakes and motives. And *still* he offered the gift of acceptance.

Have you ever wondered why the cross is the symbol of Christianity? It's a bit odd, don't you think? The cross was a means of execution, an instrument of torture. The half moon of Islam or the Jewish Star of David are a bit more cheerful, wouldn't you say?

Isn't it a bit strange that anyone would want to wear such a barbaric symbol as a piece of jewelry? What if it were a tiny gold electric chair or a silver guillotine? What's with the cross? Why is it such an important symbol for Christians? Its design is very simple. One beam stretches horizontally and the other vertically. One reaches out—like God's grace—and one stretches up to the heavens—like God's truth. One represents the breadth of God's love, and one expresses the height of his holiness. The intersection is where grace and truth meet, where God's love of humanity collides with his perfection. Jesus, the one who is fully God and fully man, brokered a deal there, taking all the sins of humanity on himself to satisfy the demands of truth while offering us grace.

A Healed Heart

The answer to our heart's loneliness is to embrace the work Jesus did for us on the cross, to receive that unconditional acceptance and love he offers us even though he knows the truth about every selfish and shameful thing we've ever done or will do. God's compassion toward us is beautifully expressed in Psalm 103:8-14:

> The LORD is merciful and gracious;
>   he is slow to get angry and full of unfailing love.
>
> He will not constantly accuse us,
>   nor remain angry forever.
>
> He has not punished us for all our sins,
>   nor does he deal with us as we deserve.
>
> For his unfailing love toward those who fear him
>   is as great as the height of the heavens above the
>   earth.
>
> He has removed our rebellious acts
>   as far away from us as the east is from the west.
>
> The LORD is like a father to his children,
>   tender and compassionate to those who fear him.

> For he understands how weak we are;
> he knows we are only dust.

As we embrace Jesus as our forgiver, he removes all the guilt and shame of our past failures. As we accept his leadership in our lives, he shows us how to relate lovingly to others—how to restore broken relationships and recognize healthy ones—and our hearts can begin to heal. I've seen it happen time and time again.

My friend Dianna was sexually abused by her father from the time she was very young. She grew up with only scattered memories of her childhood and an unexplained but powerful fear of abandonment, fear of her father, and fear of men in general. As a young mother, Dianna began to worry that she would somehow harm her own children and wondered, *Where are these thoughts coming from?*

> *Because she experienced the acceptance and forgiveness of Jesus, she forgave her father and received God's deep healing.*

One day a wise, older woman recognized Dianna's fearful behavior and announced she was coming over to talk the next day. When they met, she told Dianna about another woman's history of sexual abuse. For the first time, Dianna disclosed the fragmented memories that she now understood were snapshots of her own abuse.

Dianna's mentor led her into the understanding that the first step in her healing was to forgive her dad. By an act of her will, Dianna chose to forgive that day. Eventually she felt directed by God to write her dad a letter so that he would know he was forgiven. She knew it was a risky step. He could deny the abuse ever happened or use her vulnerability to victimize her further in some way. But Dianna knew she had to obey what she felt certain was a divine prompting and leave the results to her dad and to God.

Her father's response was better than she had dared hope for. He said, "I'm sorry. I don't deserve to be called your father."

They began to spend some time together. At first Dianna was fearful and cautious and, in her own words, "had to practice not being afraid." Though their relationship was not all that she had longed for, it was so much better than it had been before her healing began. Gradually she gained freedom from her fear and began to experience the ripples of that healing in her own marriage.

Whatever doubts I may have had about the authenticity of Dianna's healing were dispelled by the events that took place in the last few days of Dianna's dad's life. The family gathered around his bedside, and Dianna noticed that he became restless and his breathing became more labored whenever they left the room. Dianna recognized that he was drawing comfort from their nearness. So in his last few hours of life, she gave him a beautiful gift. She lay on his bed beside him to calm him all through the night.

In the morning the family returned. Dianna asked her dad, "If you could speak, what would you say to us? I'll be your voice." Believing she knew what was in his heart, she said "I love you" on his behalf to each family member present. For the first time in days, her dad's face radiated a smile. Then he turned his face away as though he saw something. Dianna asked, "What do you see? Can you see heaven and earth at the same time?" His only answer was to breathe his last.

What kindness Dianna showed to this man who had so callously betrayed her. He was a sick, old man. It would have been easy to use this opportunity to exact revenge for all the times he had abused her vulnerability as a little girl. But because she experienced the acceptance and forgiveness of Jesus, she forgave her father and received God's deep healing for the wounds her dad had inflicted. Instead of repaying him for his selfishness, she accepted what little he had to give. In return, she gave him the comfort of her nearness, understanding, and love.

Imagine how different that deathbed scene would have been for everyone involved had Dianna not chosen to forgive and allow God to heal her heart. Her dad would have died unforgiven and uncomforted. Some would say he deserved that. But Dianna's siblings would not have heard their dad's final, precious expression of love through Dianna's voice. And Dianna would still be wounded, lonely, and afraid.

God wants to heal your heart too. He wants you to look into the grace-filled eyes of Jesus and never be the same again. You can do it today. Not through your physical eyes but through spiritual eyes and in prayer. There's nothing complicated about initiating a relationship with Jesus. It is as simple as ABC. Go to Jesus in prayer, telling him you *Admit* you have sinned, you *Believe* he died to pay for your sin and rose again from the dead, and you *Choose* to let him lead you from here on in.

You may or may not feel ready to do this today. We are all at different places in our spiritual journeys. Take this great opportunity to really explore where you are and ask yourself, "Is this where I want to be?"

God created you to be most fulfilled in relationship with him and then with people. While it is scary for some of us to take the risk of trusting God (or anyone else), it is only when we are plugged in to the relationships he designed for us that we feel that sense of true belonging we all yearn for.

Notes

1. Edward M. Hallowell, M.D., *In the Human Moment* (Toronto: Random House of Canada, 1999), p. 5.
2. Ibid., pp. 8-9.

— *Plugging In* —

1. If we all want great relationships, why is it so hard to find them and then make them work?

2. How did Adam and Eve's choice to defy God change our relationship with God and others?

3. What evidence do you see in your own family of sin having entered the world?

4. What experiences have you had with past relationships that interfere with your willingness to trust in your present relationships?

5. How can we get connected to God and people in a healing, nurturing way? How can we go back to the way it was meant to be?

6. Where are you on your spiritual journey? Is this where you want to be?

7. Describe the two sides of God's character. Why do we have to experience them both to counter the contamination of sin in our relationships?

8. Why is the cross such an important symbol for Christians? What do the two components of the cross represent?

10

grasp grace

What does God really want from me?

While attending a marriage seminar on communication, Wally and his wife, Carolyn, listened to the instructor declare, "It is essential that husbands and wives know the things that are important to each other." Then he addressed the men: "Can you describe your wife's favorite flower?"

Wally leaned over, touched Carolyn's arm gently, and whispered, "White, all-purpose, isn't it?"

And thus began Wally's life of celibacy.

My husband once told me that trying to get everything right in marriage is like perfecting a golf swing. There's so much to remember. And even when you remember, it's not all that easy to do. Stick your rear end out, pull your chin in, don't stick your rear out, square your shoulders, bend your knees, don't pull your chin in, lift your head, lock your elbows, don't bend your knees. Kind of makes you wish Tiger Woods would just come and hit the ball for you, doesn't it?

For some people matters of faith are like that. Most people were raised to believe that only good people go to heaven. They live with the hope and the continual pressure to try to be good enough and do enough of the right things and avoid doing too many of the wrong things so God will let them into heaven. Since no one really knows where the threshold of acceptability is, no one with this belief system is ever sure whether the scales are tipped in his or her favor or not. Life in this paradigm is extremely stressful. Trying to live according to all the rules in the Bible is also a daunting task. Obeying the Ten Commandments is hard enough, but it gets worse. When Jesus arrived on the scene he said:

> You have heard that the law of Moses says, "Do not commit adultery." But I say, anyone who even looks at a woman with lust in his eye has already committed adultery with her in his heart (Matthew 5:27-28).

> You have heard that the law of Moses says, "Love your neighbor" and hate your enemy. But I say, love your enemies!...If you love only those who love you, what good is that? Even corrupt tax collectors do that much. If you are kind only to your friends, how are you different from anyone else? Even pagans do that. But you are to be perfect, even as your Father in heaven is perfect (Matthew 5:43-44,46-48).

Perfect. Okay. No problem, no pressure. How in this wide world are we supposed to accomplish that? As unattainable as perfection is, many people almost kill themselves trying to achieve it. They have bought into the idea that they must meet certain standards to be acceptable to themselves, to others, and to God. And so these driven people rush through life determined to be on time, look great, get promoted, keep an immaculate house...all to avoid the ever-looming cloud of failure.

They are ensnared in the performance trap. They are fueled by the belief that if they meet those unrealistic standards they've set for themselves, then and only then can they feel worthy of acceptance. The cost of internment in the performance trap is high, both for themselves and the people around them. Often manipulating other people to help them accomplish their goals, perfectionists reject those who obstruct the path to their goals, refuse to take risks to avoid failure, and leave little or no room to relax and enjoy life.

The questions that keep bumping the back of their minds are "Was it good enough?" and "Am I good enough?"

Occasionally, perfectionism still entraps me. Every once in a while I buy into the lie that I must be (or at least appear to be) competent in order to accept myself. But there was a time when perfectionism was my default position. Because of this inclination, I overprepared for speaking engagements and business meetings.

This very desire to be organized and appear competent led me to call my contact for a local speaking engagement at a mother–daughter banquet. I wanted to firm up the details and schedule a sound check for my daughter and me because we were going to be singing a duet. When we finished our business, I said to my contact, "See you at 6:30." She agreed and we hung up.

The problem was that I was thinking 6:30 the next evening. She was thinking 6:30 that evening. Somehow I had gotten the date wrong.

I took my younger daughter to kindergarten that afternoon and then went to the gym and had a really good workout. When my workout was over, there was enough time for a quick shower but not enough to wash my hair before picking her up. So there I was with sweat-crusted hair, wearing a fuzzy shirt and leggings, when I answered a frantic phone call.

"Where are you?" asked the high-pitched voice.

Adrenaline rushed through me. After listening a minute and teetering on the edge of hysteria, I hung up the phone, snatched my eldest daughter out of her warm bed, stuffed her into a dress, hurriedly dressed, called our accompanist who, mercifully, was able to come galloping over at a moment's notice, grabbed my notes, and roared across the city.

So much for a sound check and all those details I thought I was on top of. We arrived just as the group was finishing dessert. As I waited to be introduced, I thought, *I hope my slip doesn't show.* Then, *I hope I'm wearing a slip.* I looked at my daughter. She had been swimming that day and looked like a waterlogged rat, a somewhat dazed and confused waterlogged rat. As I glanced at the other little girls, I noticed the fancy little hairdos and all the special touches making them look pretty for this special night out with their moms.

That evening was very hard on the self-image of a woman caught in the performance trap. I was not on time. I did not look my best. My daughter looked like the poster child for a relief organization. I most certainly did not appear competent.

Have you had a similar experience? In his book *The Search for Significance,* Robert McGee identifies these symptoms of being caught in performance mode:

~ You become very discouraged when you fail.

~ You feel compelled to justify your mistakes.

~ You are harshly critical of yourself.

~ Fear keeps you from trying something if success isn't guaranteed.

The Approval Snare

Along with the search for perfection, there are also many people who work hard to gain the approval of others. They accept the premise that they can't survive the rejection of the important people in their lives: mothers, employers, spouses, and friends. They may even entertain the notion that if the people around them think well of them, surely God will too.

"Approval addicts" try to please others at any cost. They are usually overly sensitive to criticism and avoid people who may not approve of them. Even though they compromise unendingly and sometimes even sell out who they are and what they really want to gain acceptance, the payoff is almost always temporary and conditional. There comes a time in every relationship when we no longer sense the approval we seek. The desire for approval becomes a relentless addiction because no human being approves of us all the time. According to McGee, you may be an approval addict if:

~: You avoid people who may not approve of you.

~: You find yourself trying to impress others.

~: You become very discouraged when someone criticizes you.

~: You are uncomfortable around others who are different from you.

In the 1999 Paramount/Touchstone Pictures film *Runaway Bride*, Maggie Carpenter is a classic people pleaser. Her people-pleasing ways have earned her the dubious reputation of being a "man-eater" because she has broken the hearts of four men after leaving each of them at the marriage altar. Maggie doesn't intend to be a man-eater at all. She really cares about all her men. And as she becomes involved in each romance, she tries so hard to please the man of the moment that she becomes a relational chameleon, assuming his tastes and interests.

With Gill, "the hippie," she develops a sudden taste for tattoos, guitar music, and fried eggs. For Brian, she switches to scrambled eggs with salt, pepper, and dill. With George, the entomologist, it's bugs and poached eggs, and during the Bob era it's all about sports and garden omelets (made with egg whites only).

All Maggie's men were more interested in making her into what they wanted her to be than in finding out who she really was. That is, until she met Ike, the reporter whose initial interest in her was

> *"When I was walking down the aisle, I was walking toward someone who had no idea who I really was….I had done everything to convince him I was exactly what he wanted."*

only to expose her man-eating ways to the world. But Ike gets to know her while building his case against her. He realizes there is not a malicious bone in her body. She is simply lost.

In Ike's words, "You are so lost you don't even know what kind of eggs you like." Ike's statement is the catalyst for some soul-searching by Maggie, and she embarks on a journey to find out who she is and what she really wants out of life. In the final scenes of the movie, she realizes that she loves Ike, the one man who recognized and cared about the toll her people-pleasing pattern was taking on her. But by this point, Ike has been left in her wake of wounded, would-be grooms, so she has some convincing to do. Maggie explains, "When I was walking down the aisle, I was walking toward someone who had no idea who I really was, and it was only half the other person's fault because I had done everything to convince him I was exactly what he wanted. So it was good that I didn't go through with it because it would have been a lie. But you knew the real me." "Yes, I did," Ike agrees.

Maggie continues, "I love Eggs Benedict. I hate all the other kinds of eggs. I hate big weddings." (No doubt!) "I want to get married on a weekday when everyone is at work." Which, of course, is exactly what happens when at last she marries Ike.

Unconditional Acceptance

In the apostle John's biography of Jesus, we find another story of a runaway bride. Actually, it would be more accurate to say she was a throwaway bride. Jesus met her as he was resting by a village well while his friends went into town to buy food. The woman was there alone in the midday heat to draw water. (See John 4.)

Jesus asked the woman for a drink, which completely shocked her. It was unheard of in that first-century culture for a man—any man—to address a respectable woman who was not related to him in some way. The fact that he was Jewish and she a "hated" Samaritan made it totally surreal.

The cultural barriers of the day already broken, the way was paved for a fork-in-the-road conversation. A conversation that would change the trajectory of that woman's life.

When she replayed their dialogue in her head later that day, which I'm sure she must have done, the woman at the well probably wondered what she actually told Jesus about her life and what he seemed to already know. Her second shock of the day had been the way he had revealed the story of her life, as if he had always known her. And not just about her, but what was going on inside her.

He knew she had five failed marriages and was living with yet another man. He knew why she couldn't stand to be alone, that there was a relentless longing inside her that drove her from one relationship to another, looking for someone to accept her, to validate her, to love her. But no matter what she did, it never lasted. She couldn't please them, and they could never give her what she so desperately needed.

If this broken woman was surprised when Jesus revealed who she was, she was really amazed when he told her who *he* was. He came right out and said it: "I am the Messiah." She knew what that meant. He was the one sent from God, the one the Jewish holy books said would come to set things right in the world. That explained a lot.

This throwaway bride only spent a few minutes in Jesus' presence, but suddenly she knew that being a peak performer or a people-pleaser was not the way to gain acceptance, at least not for the long term. She realized that the only one who could offer her unconditional acceptance was God, and the only way to get it was to grasp grace. Jesus could meet her deepest needs. It wasn't about living a good life, gaining approval, being a good person, and getting it right.

Making the Grade?

> But now God has shown us a different way of being right in his sight—not by obeying the law but by the way promised in the Scriptures long ago. We are made

right in God's sight when we trust in Jesus Christ to take away our sins. And we all can be saved in this same way, no matter who we are or what we have done. For all have sinned; all fall short of God's glorious standard. Yet now God in his gracious kindness declares us not guilty. He has done this through Christ Jesus, who has freed us by taking away our sins. For God sent Jesus to take the punishment for our sins and to satisfy God's anger against us.

We are made right with God when we believe that Jesus shed his blood, sacrificing his life for us....And he is entirely fair and just in this present time when he declares sinners to be right in his sight because they believe in Jesus.

Can we boast, then, that we have done anything to be accepted by God? No, because our acquittal is not based on our good deeds. It is based on our faith. So we are made right with God through faith and not by obeying the law (Romans 3:21-28).

The Ten Commandments and the rest of the Old Testament law spelled out for us in the Bible show us the contrast between sinful humanity and a holy God. We can't possibly pull our socks up far enough to please God. We don't need to clean up our act; we need a completely new act.

When I was in college studying interior design, the process the instructors used to arrive at the grades on the projects my classmates and I submitted seemed completely random. We often wondered if they labeled the stairs with letter grades and then threw the stack of projects down the staircase, letting gravity make the decisions for them. If your project landed on the "A" stair, lucky you. If it landed further down, bummer.

I think many people envision God using a similar, though much less random, staircase system to determine where they stand. We tend to see people like Mother Teresa on the top stair, the one labeled "A+." People like Adolf Hitler are on the bottom stair, labeled "F." The rest of us are somewhere in-between. The assumption is that God has decided a certain stair is the cutoff point for entrance to heaven.

The problem is that the top stair only reaches the second floor, and God's standard is the space station. There is no way we can get there from here. We can't meet God's standard because the standard his holiness demands is perfection. And there isn't one person who hasn't sinned—not one. The best we can do is completely inadequate to God. But there is hope!

Isaiah 53:6 and the New Testament Gospels say we are like sheep that have wandered off and gotten lost. We have all gone our own way. Instead of laying the consequences of our rebellion on us, God asked Jesus to take the blame, and he willingly took it on and paid the penalty for our sins through his death on the cross. And when he hung suffering on that cross in our place, he cried, "It is finished." Our debt was *paid in full*.

Imagine you have an enormous loan from the bank. The amount you owe is like a huge pit you'll never be able to crawl out of. One day you go to the bank to pay off one month's interest. That's all you can afford to do. The bank teller brings up your account information and tells you something so shocking you have to sit down. He says that earlier that day a man came into the bank, paid your enormous debt, and deposited billions of dollars into your account.

Our Wrongs Are Erased

Through Jesus, God has not only wiped out your debt of sin and all your wrongdoing, he has also deposited into your spiritual bank account the purity, the perfection, the moral rightness of Jesus Christ. When God in heaven looks at us, he no longer sees the wrong things we've done, the things we should have done, or our failures. He sees only the absolute purity of his dearly loved son. That is what the Bible calls justification. As a result, we are completely pleasing to God. There's nothing we can do to make him love us more, and nothing we can do to make him love us less. He loves us as much as he loves Jesus.

But to enjoy this position of undeniable privilege, we have to go to the bank, claim what is now ours, and apply it to the needs in our lives. In the material realm, that might mean I pay off my Visa and buy a new car. In the spiritual realm, it means I go to God in prayer, admit my sin, accept his payment for it, and ask Jesus to be my forgiver and the leader of my life.

> *I can look back on the worst mistakes and most grievous sins in my past and know the debt they created has been paid in full. Today I do my best to live a moral life out of gratitude to God, not to win his favor.*

Just as I need to apply money to my financial needs for it to make any difference, so I need to apply the forgiveness of Jesus to my spiritual needs or I will go on striving for perfection and acceptance, and Jesus died for me in vain. Once I have accepted Jesus into my life, my debt to God is paid once and for all. And I can know without a shadow of a doubt that even when I mess up royally, miss a great opportunity, or embarrass myself, there is still someone who accepts me completely. I don't have to meet my own or anyone else's standards. I don't have to be thin, raise great kids, or hold down a job to be okay. I can leave the house with dishes on the counter, forget an appointment, and even have a bad hair day—and I don't have to beat myself up.

Why? Because my self-worth doesn't depend on meeting an artificial standard of perfection. I can look back on the worst mistakes and most grievous sins in my past and know the debt they created has been paid in full. Today I do my best to live a moral life out of *gratitude to God,* not to win his favor. Jesus has already attributed to me his right standing with God, which leaves me secure in his inexhaustible love. My worth in his eyes is firmly established. It doesn't get much better than this. This is true freedom!

— *Grasping Grace* —

1. What ideas did you grow up with regarding what it takes to get into heaven?

2. What attitudes and emotions accompanied those beliefs?

3. Describe any struggles you have with perfectionism or approval addiction.

4. What do you believe God wants from you?

5. What does justification mean? (Remember the bank story.)

6. What is one thing you can do to make God love you more?

7. What do you need to do to fully benefit from Jesus' enormous sacrifice for you?

8. "Once I have accepted Jesus into my life, my debt to God is paid once and for all. And I can know without a shadow of a doubt that even when I mess up royally, miss a great opportunity, or embarrass myself, there is still someone who accepts me completely." How do you respond to this statement?

one more thing...

Where do I go from here?

If you're like me, you're too often in a hurry. When we jump into the shower in the morning we often use two-in-one shampoo and conditioner to save time. Then we make our instant oatmeal in the microwave because, hello, the slow-cook kind takes forever. We cruise into the drive-through for our coffee and then take the expressway to get to work, returning phone calls while we drive to save time. We are multitaskers.

Upon arriving at work one morning and looking a bit disheveled, one man complained about an incident that had occurred on his morning commute. Traveling beside him on the expressway was a woman operating her vehicle with her face up close to the mirror on her visor because she was applying her eye makeup. The man looked away from the road for a few seconds, and when he brought his attention back he had just enough time to swerve dramatically to avoid hitting the woman, whose car had wandered well into his lane. The ordeal scared him so badly he dropped his vibrating electric shaver into the cup of coffee he had been balancing between his legs. The coffee splashed vociferously, scalding the vicinity of the man's legs and abruptly disconnecting his cell phone call. Having recounted the whole upsetting episode to his work partner, he then muttered, "Crazy women drivers!"

Multitasking is just one symptom of a hurried life. We live in an instant culture, and we want everything to be quick and easy. Follow these easy steps and, *voila!* problem solved. We all know life is not usually like that. There is no list of 10 simple steps, or tasks, or smart things, for that matter, that once accomplished or implemented make life work perfectly from then on. Life is complex. But like the man who ruined his shaver, his coffee, and his phone connection discovered, often the shortcuts we take in an effort to streamline our lives only make matters worse. Life is a journey, and like any journey, it is full of complications and surprises.

Interruptions and Expectations

In chapter 2 I mentioned a trip Randy and I took to Haiti. That trip was definitely full of unexpected and uncomfortable experiences. For instance, as our plane landed on the Port-au-Prince runway, I was full of anticipation and apprehension. I knew I was unprepared for what lay ahead, but I was also aware that there really was nothing I could have done to prepare my heart for the poverty and angst I would probably encounter over the next few days.

Randy and I deplaned and walked toward the terminal building. Once inside, the airport chaos erupted around us. We had been warned not to take our eyes or our hands off our luggage. The Haitian version of "red caps" hollered and grabbed at the handles of our suitcases, all vying for the tip that carrying them might produce. We did what we were told. We firmly yelled no at a decibel level we hoped could be heard over the din.

One dark-skinned hand was particularly tenacious in hanging on to our luggage. The hand's owner tugged, my husband yanked back, and the tug-of-war was on. The Haitian was shouting something at us passionately, but the combination of his Creole accent and the frenzy around us made his voice undecipherable. Finally he released our suitcase in frustration and pointed to his name tag. It read, "Ephraim Lindor, Compassion International." This man had been sent to rescue us from the chaos by helping us navigate the unfamiliar territory of Third World confusion we found ourselves in. But instead of accepting the help we so desperately needed, we had been fighting him, making it impossible for him to help us.

Once we were safely loaded into the vehicles with our luggage, we negotiated the congested streets of the capital of this small Caribbean country. The next day the adventure continued. We boarded a small, ancient Russian plane to fly to Port-de-Paix. Ephraim, our Haitian guide, was obviously nervous. *That could be explained easily enough,* we thought. *Some people just hate to fly.* That's what we hopefully decided anyway.

Then we realized that all the instrumentation on the plane was in Russian. We assumed the Haitians piloting our plane spoke Creole and possibly French or English, but probably not Russian. We finally figured out that language wasn't really a factor because the instruments apparently didn't work! As we started down the runway, the pilot slid his window open and stuck his hand out. We picked up speed, the pilot pulled his arm in, closed the window, and we took off. We don't know for certain, but we're pretty sure that's how he was measuring airspeed for take-off.

Flying over the island country was an education, providing a different perspective on the circumstances of the inhabitants. When it was time to land, our guide commented on a new safety feature of the small Port-de-Paix airport: a chain-link fence installed to keep wandering goats off the runway. Landing on the goat-free gravel runway was a jarring experience, but not nearly as turbulent as the two-hour Jeep ride to come.

The "roads" in rural Haiti would make a great test laboratory for motion sickness drugs. We were jostled all around that Jeep to the point that whatever was in our pockets was practically flying through the air. I was sitting next to a man on our team who was wearing shorts. As his bare leg bounced and rubbed against my skirted thigh, the friction started to hurt. I thought to myself, *The hair on this guy's leg is like steel wool. I've never met anyone with such coarse leg hair.*

After two hours of feeling like we'd been tumbling around like socks in the dryer, we finally arrived at Bassin Bleu, our destination. I crawled out of the Jeep and realized that my skirt was now on backward and that what had been jabbing me in the leg for the past two hours was not the hair on my friend's leg but the pin on the nametag he had tucked into the pocket of his cargo shorts.

We were a couple of hours late arriving at our final destination because we had missed our scheduled flight at the beginning of the day. (About the only thing that operates on time in Haiti is the airline.) That meant we missed supper, and we had already skipped lunch. In Haiti, you can't just stop at a fast-food outlet. Food is scarce—fast, slow, at any speed. Even if we could have found a roadside vendor, the food wouldn't have been safe for us to eat with our delicate, North American digestive systems.

> *Life is full of interruptions, surprises, detours, and pain. Daily, hourly, moment-by-moment we have to make decisions about how we will respond to the curveballs life throws at us.*

So before we went to sleep that night Randy and I used our clean pillowcases as plates, and we divided our small stash of beef jerky and trail mix into two tiny piles. I felt like we were on *Survivor*. We went to bed hungry, and as we lay awake listening to the gurgles of our stomachs, we thought how fitting it was to be able to relate in this way to such a large percentage of the population of the country who were, no doubt, lying awake listening to the same music.

Compared to the experience of my friend Heather, my time in Haiti was uneventful. Heather traveled to the poverty-stricken country with several others on a short-term mission. Their goal was to help with a small construction project. Unfortunately, all of them got dysentery. As a result, there was always a long line to use the two-seater outhouse, the only restroom they had access to. One day while Heather was awaiting her turn to use the facilities, the girl occupying one half of the outhouse suddenly had unexpected company.

She had just situated herself over the roughly cut opening, hovering to avoid unnecessary contact with the less-than-sanitary facilities, when out of the hole beside her jumped a huge rat. The unwelcome rodent flew through the air and landed on the poor girl's lap. Heather, and those in line with her, heard a terrible scream emanating from the outhouse, followed immediately by thumping noises. The door flew open and a hysterical girl stumbled awkwardly from the tiny building with her pants still around her ankles. No one knows what happened to the rat.

When traveling to a place like Haiti, you've got to know you're in for some new experiences. But we didn't expect to fly in a rattle-trap of a plane and land on a rough, rutted runway recently purged of goats. We didn't know we would have our brains scrambled in a Jeep or that we would go to bed hungry. I'm sure Heather expected some challenges, but she didn't expect dysentery. Her teammate knew she wouldn't have long in the latrine by herself, but she certainly didn't expect a lap-dancing rat.

Life is like that too, isn't it? Full of interruptions, surprises, detours, and pain. Generous helpings of what we didn't expect and often not as much of what we were hoping for. Life is a journey. The struggles, surprises, and interruptions of life are constant. Daily, hourly, moment-by-moment decisions about how we will live, what is important to us, and what we will strive for have to be made. How will we respond to all the curveballs life throws at us?

Diversion or Expedition?

We can set a course based on an objective set of values or we can stagger from event to event making it up as we go along. If we deliberately chart a course drawing on what we know and wisdom beyond our own, we can get somewhere. But if we refuse that help, life has the potential to become much more turbulent. We might arrive at the end of our journey with regret and futility.

Sociologist Tony Campolo talks about a study in which 50 people over the age of 95 were asked one question: "If you could live your life over again, what would you do differently?" It was an open-ended question that invited all kinds of answers. But one theme emerged: "If I could do life over again, I would reflect more on what life is all about."

There are two basic approaches to life. One is based on doing whatever feels good at the moment, on whatever makes us happy and makes the pain go away. Let's call this approach *diversion*. The other is to set a direction and chart a course based on our values and convictions and to doggedly pursue it despite hardship and challenges. Let's call this approach *expedition*.

Like a shortcut that ends up complicating your day by costing you time and aggravation, the diversion approach to life is much easier in the short-term, but then usually gets harder. For example, we fail to get up in time to make ourselves presentable, so we do it in the car and spill coffee all over ourselves while swerving to avoid the guy shaving in the next lane. We jump into a relationship or job or parenthood without adequate value-driven preparation and end up in crisis.

We start expeditions with preparation. Almost every decision is made deliberately with the objective and destination in mind. This requires self-discipline and sometimes self-denial, but in the end we have a smoother path.

Following the Footprints

During the era of slavery in the United States, many slaves escaped their bondage and fled to the "Free States" or Canada. Because they were denied education, including any significant knowledge of geography, the slaves couldn't plan an escape route. Many knew only that somewhere out there was a place, if one could survive the journey, where a person of color could live with dignity and freedom. Most knew that the North Star pointed the way to that place. The star became their symbol of hope and freedom. But with such vague plans, many were walking into impassable or dangerous terrain. Often they were recaptured or died of exposure.

Members of the Underground Railroad were aware of the difficulties awaiting the escaped slaves. Around the year 1831, the Railroad began to send travelers into the South to secretly teach slaves safe routes of escape, using the North Star for navigation. Employing the African oral tradition of reporting factual information through music, the slaves repeated the escape route directions to their children and to each other in songs. Many of the Negro spirituals, now appreciated all over the world, were actually coded routes of escape. The slaves could fearlessly sing their songs to inform and inspire one another right under their masters' noses without arousing suspicion.

One such coded song is *Follow the Drinking Gourd*. The escape route out of Alabama and Mississippi is described, beginning with the handle of the Big Dipper, which points to the North Star. The constellation looked to the slaves like the gourd they drank from in the fields; hence, the name of the song.

The directions for this escape route were brought to the slaves by a man known only as Peg Leg Joe. Joe was an itinerant carpenter who spent his winters in the South going from plantation to plantation describing the way to freedom. The song describes how the distinctive footprints left by an artificial limb marked the route to the North. The song even tells the slaves what time of year to begin the journey and what landmarks to watch for along the way:

> *When the sun comes back and the first quail calls,*
> *Follow the Drinking Gourd*
> *The old man is a-waitin' for to carry you to freedom,*
> *Follow the Drinking Gourd*
>
> *The river bed makes a mighty fine road,*
> *Dead trees to show you the way*
> *And its left foot, peg foot, traveling on*
> *Follow the Drinking Gourd*

The river ends between two hills
Follow the Drinking Gourd
There's another river on the other side,
Follow the Drinking Gourd

Where the great big river meets the little river,
Follow the Drinking Gourd
For the old man is a-waitin' to carry you to freedom if you
Follow the Drinking Gourd

Quail are migratory birds that winter in the South. These words were telling the slaves to wait until winter to travel. To escape, most slaves had to cross the Ohio River. Since the journey to freedom took most escapees an entire year, the Railroad recommended travelers begin their flight in the winter in order to reach the Ohio the following winter. This timing solved a significant problem: The river was too wide and swift to swim across; a winter crossing enabled slaves to walk across on the ice.

> *The path to true freedom is following Jesus' directions and abandoning destructive choices.*

The dead trees along the route were marked (by burning or carving) with the distinctive footprint pattern of Peg Leg Joe, helping the slaves distinguish the correct path.

Freedom promised a life free of brutality, servitude, and chains for the man or woman courageous enough to leave the familiar behind. We have some things in common with the fugitive slaves. We too need a clear destination and directions for getting there or we'll end up wasting our opportunities to live lives of freedom and fulfillment. And we too have chains. You may be thinking, *Okay, I understand the part about the need for a clear destination, but I am not anyone's slave. I don't have chains.*

Jesus had a conversation with a group of his followers about this very thing. He told them that the path to true freedom was in following the directions he had been teaching them and abandoning their destructive choices and behaviors. The conversation is recorded for us in John's biography of Jesus:

> Jesus said to the people who believed in him, "You are truly my disciples if you keep obeying my teachings. And you will know the truth, and the truth will set you free."

> "But we are descendants of Abraham," they said. "We have never been slaves to anyone on earth. What do you mean, 'set free'?"

> Jesus replied, "I assure you that everyone who sins is a slave of sin. A slave is not a permanent member of the family, but a son is part of the family forever. So if the Son sets you free, you will indeed be free" (John 8:31-36).

We all have sinful, self-defeating behaviors we need to break free of to be all we were created to be. For some, the chains are a poor self-image that keeps them from moving forward. The recordings that echo in their heads keep their feet planted on territory hostile to self-acceptance. For many women, the chains are the tyranny of an overcrowded life. Others are trapped by their need to control everyone and everything around them instead of trusting God. Still others wear chains of discontent that prevent them from getting to a place of "enough."

Too many women are at the mercy of their emotions, relentlessly controlled by anger, frustration, or fear. Some are shackled to an abusive past with chains of unforgiveness. Some are imprisoned by loneliness.

Following in the footsteps of Jesus and navigating according to the directions he's given us in the Bible sets us on the path to an expansive life of satisfaction and joy. Knowing the truth and acting on it is key. According to Jesus, it's the *only* way. He said, "I am the way, the truth, and the life. No one can come to the Father except through me" (John 14:6). The apostle Paul echoed this declaration in a letter to his young friend Timothy: "For there is only one God and one Mediator who can reconcile God and people. He is the man Christ Jesus. He gave his life to purchase freedom for everyone" (1 Timothy 2:5).

We can try to find our own way if we want to, if we think we or someone else knows better. Jesus certainly won't force himself and his wisdom on us. But striking out on our own will turn out a lot like a runaway slave wandering in the general vicinity of the North without directions and without any idea of the terrain or the dangers ahead.

A Life of Hope

Entering into a relationship with Jesus whereby we allow him to guide us through life doesn't guarantee us unending happiness. But it does make freedom from the fallout of destructive decisions possible. It gives us hope and the strength to persevere and gain something positive in all situations.

My friend Patty has lived her life both ways. Through her childhood and early adulthood she was on her own. She never really heard about Jesus and his teachings in a way that made sense to her. These are the words she uses to describe her life *before* she decided to follow Jesus:

Rejection	Brokenness
Loneliness	Poor
Lack of direction	Betrayal
Sexual abuse	Colossal disappointment
Mental abuse	Insecure
Abandonment	Fatherless
Death	Sexuality struggles
Smoking habit	Parental abuse

Drugs	Lack of adult input
Sin	Anger
Rage	Boundary-less
Resentment	Doormat
Weakness	Bitterness
Lack of judgment	Ugliness
Darkness	Powerless
No identity	Guns
Bad choices	Fear
Sad	Wounded
Pain	Heartaches
Walled	Scared
Low self-esteem	Prostitution
Scarred	Alcoholism
Violence	Adultery
Chameleon	Friendless
Police intervention	Purposeless

In the midst of this dark, depressing, and lonely life, God sent an emissary sort of like Peg Leg Joe. Someone to show her the way out of her prison of despair. Both Patty and her husband, Marshall, came into relationship with Jesus Christ through this person's influence. They connected to a small group for new believers and were like human sponges. It was through this small group that Patty first learned about heaven. She discovered that eternal life was part of the deal she signed up for when she invited Jesus into her life. Her response? She said, "No way! You mean I get all this and heaven too?" She was so grateful to be saved from her ugly life on earth that to find out God still had more for her was almost too much to take in.

As Patty matured spiritually, she became aware of many ways the scars on her soul were affecting the way she lived her life and related to people, especially to her husband. Through counseling, classes, and relationships available in her new Christian community, she learned to make better choices that healed the hurts of the past. She learned she had gifts and abilities to offer others, and she began to share them. Eventually her natural leadership ability emerged, and she took on roles where her influence helped women progress through the stages of growth and healing she had experienced since inviting Jesus to forgive her for her failures and take leadership in her life.

Following Jesus' path enabled Patty to build a better life. These are the words she uses to describe her life now:

Peace	Jesus
Boundaries	God-directed
Confidence	Unconditional love
Discernment	Life purpose
Light	Truth
Known identity	Grace
Joy	Transparent
Security	Self-control
Supernatural healing	Forgiveness
Prayer	Relationships
Family	Blameless
Without condemnation	Holy
God's child	Woman
Guidance	Worship
Mentors	Overcomer
Victory	Warrior

Wholeness	Scar tissue
Foundation	Marriage redeemed
Leadership	Spiritual gifts
Father	Friends
Contentment	Beauty
Strong character	Integrity
God-fearing	Authority
Commitment	Happiness

Patty's story is pretty dramatic. Not everyone has such obvious chains. You may never have suffered abuse or known the humiliation of police intervention in your home. But maybe you are aware of a certain "stuckness" in unhealthy patterns. You may have a sense of wandering aimlessly over unfamiliar terrain. Peg Leg Joe entered into the

It's time to choose a course. Be bold, be proactive. Follow the footprints of Jesus. You'll never regret it!

misery of the American slaves to show them a way to freedom. Jesus entered the human race to do the same thing. But he went much further. He became a slave. In Paul's letter to the Philippians we read:

Though he [Jesus] was God, he did not demand and cling to his rights as God. He made himself nothing; he took the humble position of a slave and appeared in human form. And in human form he obediently humbled himself even further by dying a criminal's death on a cross (Philippians 2:6-8).

Be Bold!

Jesus' love is so immense, so powerful, so personal, that he chose slavery for himself to set you free. You personally. There is love in heaven with your name on it. No one was meant for slavery of any kind. We were created for so much more. And when we follow in the footsteps of our deliverer and travel through this life according to his directions (as expressed in the Bible), we are led out of our private bondage. We begin walking toward the spectacular life God promised and created us for.

In the opening pages of this book I wrote, "The quality of the choices we make today will be reflected in the quality of our lives tomorrow." I invite you to take a moment to assess the progress you've made on your spiritual journey. Reflect on the choices you've made along the way while considering the 10 smart things I've highlighted in this book. Ask yourself: "Am I where I want to be on my spiritual journey?" "Am I ready to embrace Jesus as the one to guide me through life?" "Am I ready to make space, manage emotions, concede control, live generously, resolve relationships, accept myself, conquer discontentment, offload stress, plug in, and grasp grace to improve my life?"

Living passively leads to disappointment. It's time to choose a course. Be bold, be proactive. Follow the footprints of Jesus and move forward. You'll never regret it!

— *Following Jesus' Footsteps* —

1. As you look back on your journey, what interruptions, struggles, and surprises have taken your life a different direction than you anticipated?

2. Have you ever taken a shortcut only to find the "easy way" complicated your life?

3. Which term best describes your life: diversion or expedition? Why?

4. In what areas of your life are you in chains?

5. "Jesus' love is so immense, so powerful, so personal, that he chose slavery for himself to set you free. There is love in heaven with your name on it. When we follow in the footsteps of our deliverer and travel through this life according to his directions, we are led out of bondage and walk toward the spectacular life God promised and created us for." Have you experienced this? What is your response to this passionate statement?

6. List 10 words or phrases that describe your life right now.

7. Now list 10 words or phrases that describe how you would like your life to be.

8. What, if anything, is preventing you from inviting Jesus to be your guide on the life journey you describe in question 7? What can you do about it?

9. Have you invited Jesus into your life? If not and you're ready to take this important step, use your own words to ask Jesus to forgive the wrongs of your past and to guide you into the future he has planned for you.

Welcome to God's family! Share your new path with a close friend or someone at a Bible-based church. If you desire more information or spiritual help, send an e-mail to questions@straighttalk.ab.ca.

About the Author

Donna Carter has a unique ability to synthesize life experience into positive life lessons. She is much sought-after as a speaker in Canada and the United States because of her clarity, humor, and the lightbulb moments she triggers for women seeking help on their spiritual journeys.

Donna lives in Alberta, Canada, with her husband, Randy, who is a youth speaker, and their two teenage daughters, Kendall and Kevann. Having studied and worked as an interior designer for 26 years, Donna now devotes her career life to helping women build better lives.

The Carters work for Straight Talk Ministries, a nonprofit organization they founded in 1994 to pursue their passion of helping people find faith and apply it to everyday life.

Donna and Randy may be contacted through Straight Talk Ministries:

Website: www.straighttalk.ab.ca
E-mail: admingirl@telus.net
Phone: 1-866-835-5827

Since 1999, the Carters have also been involved in partnership with Compassion International. They are passionate about this organization's mandate of "releasing children from poverty in Jesus' name." Compassion partners with local churches to raise up individuals who will one day be world changers themselves. Through Compassion's one-on-one sponsorship ministry, hundreds of thousands of children in countries all over the world receive practical help, hope for the future, and opportunities to break the cycle of poverty.

If you would like to join Randy and Donna in this important and fulfilling work by sponsoring a child, contact Compassion by clicking on the Compassion link on the Straight Talk website.

Experience 10 Smart Things
with Your Friends

10 Smart Things Women Can Do to Build a Better Life is available as a fun, life-management video course perfect for churches and church outreaches. You and your group will discover valuable tools to help you successfully navigate life. While exploring and offering practical suggestions on real-life topics, author and teacher Donna Carter gently brings to life the truth that it is only when we are in a transformational relationship with the God who created us that we can live life to the fullest.

The "Group Study Kit" contains:

- 1 Leader's Guide (this book)
- 1 Participant's Guide*
- 2 DVDs that include ten 20-minute teaching segments, a leaders' session, and a promo clip

  * To order additional leader's and participant's guides, go to www.10smartthings.com.

What people are saying about *10 Smart Things*

"To communicate our faith effectively, we need bridges between our world and the world of the not-yet-convinced. This course is such a bridge."

DR. STEVE WILE, director of ministry
Billy Graham Evangelistic Association of Canada

"Like Donna herself, this course is approachable and safe—a great first step on a great spiritual journey."

ROBYN K. MANNING, spiritual formation pastor,
First Alliance Church, Calgary, Canada

**For more information on the course
or to place your order, go to**

www.10smartthings.com

or call

1-866-835-5827

More Great Books from Harvest House Publishers

THE POWER OF A PRAYING® WOMAN
Stormie Omartian

Stormie's deep knowledge of Scripture and candid examples from her own prayer life will help you trust God with your deep longings (not just your pressing needs), cover every area of your life with prayer, and maintain a right heart before God. Includes heartfelt prayers to help and encourage you as you draw closer to God.

GOT TEENS?
Jill Savage and Pam Farrel

Jill Savage, founder of Hearts at Home Ministries, and Pam Farrel, cofounder of Masterful Living Ministries, offer commonsense solutions, insightful research, and creative ideas to help you guide your children successfully through the sometimes rough teen years. You'll discover how to serve as a defender, a shepherd, a CEO, and 12 other vital roles that come with having teens in the house. Discover the special needs your child will have and how to help him or her reach adulthood successfully.

RED-HOT MONOGAMY
Bill and Pam Farrel

The Farrels candidly reveal truths about sexual relationships and what husbands and wives need to know to keep passion burning: How a little skill turns marriage into red-hot monogamy, how sex works best emotionally and physically, and how to avoid the "pleasure thieves" that steal fulfillment. Difficult-to-discuss topics and biblical principles are presented with sensitivity and fun. Perfect for newlyweds, long-time couples, and those in between.

SMALL CHANGES FOR A BETTER LIFE
Elizabeth George

Don't settle for okay when best is in sight! Are you *almost* happy? Is success just out of reach? Whether your life needs minor adjustments or a major overhaul, beloved author Elizabeth George helps you pinpoint problem areas and then reveals the small changes you can make to transform your life into one of greater achievement, contentment, and joy. Using the Bible as a guide, Elizabeth explores how to find fulfillment and excel in your relationships, friendships, spiritual life, and more. Seek—and achieve!—God's best for your life.

STONECROFT®
MINISTRIES

Stonecroft Ministries equips and encourages women
of every age, every stage, and every face
to impact their communities
with the Gospel of Jesus Christ.

Our life-changing, faith-building resources include:

- *Stonecroft Biblical Training Tools* including **AWARE** Evangelism
(**A**lways **W**atching **A**nd **R**esponding with **E**ncouragement)

- *Stonecroft Bible Studies* designed to guide those who do not yet
know Jesus Christ as Savior, and believers, simply, yet profoundly, into a rich relationship with Him—the One who has
so much to say to them

- *Stonecroft Life Publications* which clearly explain the Gospel
through stories of people whose lives have been impacted by
Jesus Christ

- *Outreach Groups* (such as Women's Connections, Moms on
the Run, Vital Network, and Pray & Play) tailored to meet the
needs of local communities

- *Events* such as the October 2, 2010 international **Impact '10**
and Leaders Live! to equip women in evangelism, prayer, and
leadership

- *Stonecroft's web site*—stonecroft.org—offering fresh content
daily to equip and encourage you to impact your communities with the Gospel of Jesus Christ

Stonecroft Staff serve you via dedicated
and enthusiastic **Field Directors** stationed across
the United States, plus a Home Office team, overseeing the
leadership of tens of thousands of dedicated volunteers.

Contact us at connections@stonecroft.org or (800) 525-8627,
and visit stonecroft.org to learn more about these and other
outstanding Stonecroft resources, groups, and events.

Women connecting with God, each other, and their communities